BRITISH LITERATURE SINCE 1945

Also by George Watson

THE ENGLISH IDEOLOGY
POLITICS AND LITERATURE IN MODERN BRITAIN
THE DISCIPLINE OF ENGLISH
THE STORY OF THE NOVEL
THE LITERARY CRITICS
WRITING AND THESIS
THE CERTAINTY OF LITERATURE
THE NEW CAMBRIDGE BIBLIOGRAPHY OF
   ENGLISH LITERATURE (*general editor*)
THE SHORTER NEW CAMBRIDGE BIBLIOGRAPHY
   OF ENGLISH LITERATURE (*general editor*)

British Literature since 1945

George Watson

Fellow of St John's College, Cambridge

St. Martin's Press   New York

© George Watson 1991

All rights reserved. For information, write:
Scholarly and Reference Division,
St. Martin's Press, Inc., 175 Fifth Avenue,
New York, N.Y. 10010

First published in the United States of America in 1991

Printed in Great Britain

ISBN 0–312–05339–8

Library of Congress Cataloging-in-Publication Data
Watson, George, 1927–
British literature since 1945 / George Watson.
    p.   cm.
Includes bibliographical references and index.
ISBN 0–312–05339–8
1. English literature—20th century—History and criticism.
I. Title.
PR471.W28   1991
820.9'00914—dc20   90–43361
                                                         CIP

for Richard Luckett

Contents

Preface and Acknowledgements

This argumentative study of the literature of a single island in a single age was written because there is nothing like it, and I thought it might be time there was.

In the 1970s I took to lecturing in Cambridge (and elsewhere) on British literature since 1945 – partly because it looked like an interesting gap to be filled, whether in my home university, abroad in the European Community, or in North America – and more specifically because academia can easily suffer from an arrested sense of modernity, confusing it with Modernism, and it sometimes needs to be told about the glories of recent times. Names stick and do damage; and once a literary movement of the 1910s became known as Modernism, there were always likely to be those, a half-century on and more, who perseveringly thought it must be the latest thing, and they may still need to be shown how anti-modern it is. Eliot, Pound and Joyce published most of their writings before anyone now in his working life was born; and modern literature, it may be worth insisting, did not end with the death of D. H. Lawrence in 1930, with T. S. Eliot's *Four Quartets* in 1943, or with the plays and novels of an expatriate Irishman in Paris called Samuel Beckett. Harold Pinter already looks a better dramatist than Eliot, and as good as Beckett; Iris Murdoch, among others who gave new life to realistic fiction at about the time of the coronation of Elizabeth II in 1953, as considerable a novelist as Lawrence and better than Virginia Woolf. Such, at least, were among the reflections born of a stirring discontent with the continuing prestige of a dilapidated Modernist cult in the academic teaching of literature. The polemics of Evelyn Waugh and George Orwell, meanwhile, that emerged powerfully in the anti-totalitarian mood of the war against Hitler and the opening of his death-camps in the spring and summer of 1945, struck me as unjustly faded from memory, blanded away by biographers and, by now, remote enough from our own affluent and unapocalyptic age to have become either neglected or radically misunderstood.

The book began, then, as an act of partisanship. I believe the age of the second Elizabeth to have been one of the great ages of the British arts, and humbly share the view of some of its best critics – of William Empson, for example, and Philip Larkin – that the decay of Modernism in Britain before and during the Second World War was a shift of mind to be welcomed and applauded. This has been a half-century marked by a civil war between old-style Modernism and new-style realism, with realism winning: a victory to be applauded on all sorts of grounds, as I believe, and not just literary, since realism is a way of looking hard at the world; and a nation needs to look hard at itself, and report on what it sees, if it is ever purposefully to grow and change. When England changes, as that sympathetic Frenchman André Siegfried once remarked, people say that she is dying, and it is never true. The point is wide-ranging. There have been plenty since the war to say that the novel is dying – or poetry, or the theatre. Some critics love the smell of death. But change is as natural to the system as revolution and stagnation are unnatural to it; and it is not, of itself, alarming. In fact a tradition needs to change in order to preserve itself and its past. Change is less a way of being different than a means of survival and a way of staying alive and afloat.

That, in all likelihood, is a view commoner among novelists, playwrights and poets than among academic critics: which is why the un-Modernist case may now be usefully recast, as I have tried to do here, in academic terms. The creative intelligence is always the first to know, which is why it creates. In that sense, as I once tried to show in *The Literary Critics*, it is often more critical than the critics, who are by duty and calling concerned with the works of other ages, and who sometimes confuse complexity with profundity, technicality with rigour, and well-publicised disputes about critical theory at international conferences with the life of mind. They easily confuse ideas, above all, especially if neatly packaged and labelled, with thought itself: Modernism with modernity, structuralism and its intellectual heirs with the latest thing, and Marxist theories of history with the way the world is going. Such incidents have done higher education little credit in recent years, and I have already dealt with some recent critical theories in a book called *The Certainty of Literature*. It is astonishing that students, and even some of those who teach them, should be surprised to learn that Karl Marx was a year older than Queen Victoria – a contemporary, as a thinker, of Gladstone and John Stuart Mill; or that 'semiotic', a word mentioned by John Locke in his *Essay* of 1690, was a term known to the eighteenth century. It is not nostalgics among us who are old-fashioned but the avant-garde. While everything around it changes, it somehow strenuously contrives to stay more or less the same.

The creative harvest of Britain since 1945 is huge. With so much to be sifted, the book has been above all a labour of love – sometimes touched, as love-affairs often are, with a sense of the frantic and sudden attacks of exasperated despair. I have been lucky to have had the chance to deliver it – or bits of it – in a university that has allowed me to speak my mind for thirty years, in a faculty usually tolerant of diversity and in a college

unfailing in its kindness. Lucky, too, in a deeper way: to
have lived through what I here describe, to have read
such books and seen such plays when they were new,
and with the shocked and comprehending eye of the
contemporary. (One has to comprehend, after all, in
order to be shocked.) A pity no one in the age of the first
Elizabeth, so far as anyone knows, ever attempted
anything like it. This is a book by a contemporary about
a nation in its literary aspect, and in a highly fertile age.
The arts in that age stand high – some, it may be, even
higher than literature, and if the book had been about
music I should unhesitatingly have called it the greatest
age of all, Benjamin Britten and Michael Tippett having
made British music in recent times second to none. In
literature it may still be seen as among the greatest: not
the equal of the first Elizabeth's, but more distinguished
and abundant than that of most of her successors: the
best for drama, I suspect, since Shakespeare died, for
the novel since the age of Charles Dickens and George
Eliot, for polemical prose absolutely. And since critics
are supposed to have a point of view and declare it, I
may add that Ian Fleming, though not a better writer
than Virginia Woolf, by now looks a more compelling
story-teller, George Orwell as remarkable a stylist, in his
own way, as Samuel Beckett, Dylan Thomas's *Deaths and
Entrances* (1946) the finest book of verse by a British-born
poet to appear since the war, and William Empson's
Argufying (1987) the best miscellany of criticism in
English in any age whatever. Such views are not expected to meet with general assent, but at least no one
can say he has not been warned.

The book, in any case, is not – or not necessarily –
about the best, and I am vividly conscious of how much
I have not read, of how much I may have read and
forgotten. Historians rightly love the problematical. I
have favoured problems and issues here as much as

great names, and am far from offering, even by the remotest implication, a list of recommended reading. Of course some unmentioned works are easily better than some that are mentioned. The book, in short, is more analytic than annalistic. It is too soon for an annal. As for the total shape of the argument, it groups together what seems most naturally to group, and the book is built as a series of debates rather than a synopsis or a chronology. The novel, the theatre, even the short poem, are natural areas of critical debate. Other chapters concern the temper and obsessions of the time, and I have simply let them happen, as I wrote, and ignored the harsh call of consistency. An age is a various and untidy thing; an age one has lived through, irremediably so.

The scope of the book is severely insular, and it deals with writers native to or mainly resident in Great Britain since 1945. That is not because Britain is an island or because the book is the work of a nationalist. I am among the growing number who, even before the belated entry of Britain into the European Community in January 1973, believed its days of unlimited sovereignty are numbered and hope that they are. That does not alter the fact that, for a literary historian, Britain represents a convenient entity to be explored and pondered.

This is a study of differences in similarities, of similarity in differences. If the book is organised, on the whole, by literary kinds or by groups and coteries, I hope too that a sense of background, social and political – one small, interesting island strategically situated off the north-west coast of Holland – has never entirely vanished from view. Even Ulster is not here, being plainly worth a book of its own, especially for its poetry. Insularity is nothing to be ashamed of. For most of human history, after all, it has been easier to travel by sea than by land, and for millennia the ocean has not locked Britain in but given her the earth to wander in.

That is the dimension of space. As for time, the book is the panorama of an age, and of a long age, not the snapshot of a moment. Even recent history is a kind of history, and all knowledge is of past time. The book has no end-date and could have none, but I hope 1945 will be readily accepted as a starting-point, and one that gives less trouble than any other in living memory would do. Some figures are excluded simply by dates; others by departure. James Joyce and Virginia Woolf died in 1941, for example, and T. S. Eliot stopped writing poems (though not plays) at much the same time. They are too early. Famous expatriates, meanwhile, like Robert Graves, soon to resettle in Spain, or W. H. Auden and Christopher Isherwood self-exiled in the United States, decided by 1945 not to live here except on a visit, and they too are omitted. So much seems clear. Some figures, admittedly, fall awkwardly across the date-line of 1945, and here I have yielded to instinct and allowed a general sense of their writings to rule. Ivy Compton-Burnett and Graham Greene seem to me inescapably 1930s writers, like Richard Hughes and Joyce Cary – however much they may have written since the war. Tolkien, by contrast, though born as early as 1892 and three years older than Robert Graves, is plainly a post-war phenomenon, however long it may have taken him to conceive and write *The Lord of the Rings* (1954–5). Evelyn Waugh and George Orwell are neatly bisected by the Great Peace of 1945, as authors; but since *Brideshead Revisited* and *Animal Farm* appeared simultaneously in that very year, I have devoted a chapter to those authors and those works as an overture. The important thing, as William Empson used to say, is for a critic not to be bother-headed.

Post-war Britain is a rich, sparky culture, and it has

already lasted as long as the age that separates *Hamlet* from Milton's *Poems* of 1645, or *Lyrical Ballads* from *Martin Chuzzlewit*. That is no small bite, and it goes without saying that I have bitten off more than I should ever wish to swallow or even chew. Perhaps, when the chronicle of the age is told at due length and in all its fullness, the perspectives will have changed, and few enough of my judgements will stand. So be it. This is an interim report and no more. But at least something has been set in motion and a start made.

ACKNOWLEDGEMENTS

British literature since the war has been wonderfully served, and in astonishingly quick time, by reference-books and studies. Two works of reference deserve special tribute: I. R. Willison, *The New Cambridge Bibliography of English Literature volume 4: 1900–50* (1972), which deals with writers of the British Isles established by 1950 and their secondary materials; and David C. Sutton, *Location Register of Twentieth-Century English Literary Manuscripts and Letters*, 2 vols (1988), published by the British Library.

For the rest I can give only brief and passing thanks here to a medley of books that have helped in various ways beyond the scope of individual chapters, and not only in literary ways. The fourth volume of George Orwell, *Collected Essays, Journalism and Letters* (1968), is a literary chronicle of 1945–50 composed at the time; while Bernard Levin, *The Pendulum Years* (1970), deals combatively with the 1960s. *Age of Austerity 1945–51*, edited by Michael Sissons and Philip French (1963), assembles essays on the Attlee period; *Declaration*, edited by Tom Maschler (1957), essays by Angry Young Writers of the 1950s including John Osborne and Colin

Wilson, to be answered by Anthony Hartley in *A State of England* (1963). Meanwhile Anthony Sampson, *Anatomy of Britain* (1962, revised 1983), is a dissection of politics and society in post-war years; and Bernard Bergonzi, *The Situation of the Novel* (1970), debates some of the new dilemmas of British fiction.

That is to scratch the surface, and it deals only with what one may happen to have read. Reading is after all only a part of a literary life, and not always the greatest part; and my debt to theatre-visits and to conversations with authors, and about them, exceeds (I suspect) even my debt to books and periodicals. But then when it comes to conversation, and the maturing fruits of conversation, I do not begin to understand how to acknowledge what I owe, or to whom. At least, however, I know how much I owe to Miss Josephine Richardson, who typed; to E. E. Duncan-Jones; and to the dedicatee, with whom I have shared a memorable Cambridge seminar on the literature of the twentieth century.

GEORGE WATSON

You are a curious people: . . . conscious, as you walk in the sun, of the length or shortness of the shadows that you cast.

Paul Scott, *The Jewel in the Crown* (1966)

1

Crusoe's Island

The image of the island is to be found and cherished, above all, in the stories it has told about itself, and perhaps believed of itself, for nearly half a century since it emerged into the troubled and hungry peace of 1945.

It is an image, by and large, that coheres and satisfies. Crusoe's fabled isle contained all he needed to sustain life – given, that is, that he had rescued so much of use from the wreck, not forgetting a Bible; and Defoe's most compelling point was that the island is a self-sufficient place to anyone who can bring courage to the task of living in it, along with an inherited faith and a few tools. Britain since 1945 has proved much like that, though not altogether like that. It brought ashore from the near-disaster of Hitler's war the survivals of a long literary past, including the longest of all theatrical traditions in human history, and found some surprisingly untraditional uses for them, as Crusoe once did for his tool-kit: most notably the fictional realism that Defoe's novel about a marooned sailor, in 1719, once made the inspiration of all Europe. It has lived, among other things, a life of intricate self-contemplation, rather like Crusoe keeping calendar of the days and weeks and faithfully observing in solitude the ancient usages of his tribe. As one of its authors and artists, a London Welshman, once remarked, Britain is 'necessarily insular',[1] as if its bordering of ocean were somehow intrinsic to it and essential to its whole being. It has watched its own health, too, both physical and spiritual, with an attentive and critical self-reverence. It has regarded itself solemnly, satirically, whimsically, respectfully. And an age of empire past, it has waited for the world to come to it.

No vain hope, as it happens, for (as to Crusoe) the world came. It is doubtful if, even in the nineteenth century, the power of the British literary mind over the earth has ever been greater than in the late twentieth century. Its language, after 1945, suddenly became the lingua franca of the world – the first mankind has ever known – and more than half of the world's mail, it is said, is now in English. Its theatre, since the mid 1950s, has been widely acknowledged the world's wonder. Its fiction is vast, and vastly translated. Its journalism and its polemical tradition, whether in politics or in the arts, is unignorable, its broadcasting the world's delight. Only its poetry, composed in a minor key, is (for better or worse) widely disregarded. In a post-imperial age it has shown a vitality more than sufficient to live to itself.

That self-sufficiency is literary; and literature, it seems clear, easily outpaces most other national endeavours. In no other respect is Britain effectively insular. Its economy, as a world trader, is sensitive to every trade wind that blows. Its defence has been largely the concern of other powers since the fall of Singapore in 1942; and the British independent nuclear deterrent is no more than a phrase, since it is not independent and, as the Falklands crisis of 1982 showed, it does not deter. Its policies, domestic and foreign – not least its tardy entry into the European Community in January 1973 – have been largely a belated reaction to the original achievements of others. Its political system is antiquated, compared with its neighbours, and it enjoys in free Europe the melancholy distinction of boasting no government since the war to represent the majority will. Its public welfare, heralded as a prospect unique on earth when Parliament accepted the Beveridge report in 1943, was in relative decline as early as the 1950s before its continental rivals; its industrial growth so slow that by the 1970s it was the poorest member of the Community, as it then was, excepting only Ireland and Italy.

Its literary pre-eminence, then, is extraordinary: not just in its sudden and easy victory over such historical rivals as France and the United States but in itself. Britain annually publishes three times as many titles, relative to population, as the United States; and most books published in Britain sell abroad, if calculated as to copies. European cities receive its acting companies as theatrical revelations, never questioning that London is the theatre-capital of the world. It was not always so, even in recollection. And all that is utterly unlike the slow decline of many of its services and manufactures, and utterly unlike the endless, indecisive bickering of politicians elected on minority votes and representing, all too often, the declining powers of sectional interests in unions and industry.

The sufficiency of British literature is almost as re-markable if contrasted with the other arts. London is the great city of art auctions, with New York; but it has never in this century rivalled Paris or New York as a place for painters and sculptors to live in. Since Edward Elgar's first symphony in 1908, British music has en-joyed its greatest age; but in international reputation it has made Britain little more than one musical nation among many. The British film, intermittently lively as a creative form, has seldom contrived to free itself, for long, of a humiliating dependence on foreign capital. Broadcasting is pre-eminent, at least in the ever-creative medium of radio; but television borrows from abroad as much as it creates at home. The Crusoe syndrome is largely confined to the printed book, then, and in part to theatre. In most other matters, since 1945, Britain has been effectively a dependent state, whether in peace or in war, and the dominance of British fiction across the world is unmatched by almost everything else, though some might hopefully seek exceptions in education, broadcasting and financial services like marine insurance.

The Crusoe syndrome, as I have dared to call it, is nowhere absolute, and British literature since 1945 has succumbed to occasional, and occasionally catastrophic, influences from outside itself. In 1955 London theatre saw Samuel Beckett's *Waiting for Godot*, a play composed first in French and later in English by a detribalised Irishman living in Paris, and theatrical minimalism was suddenly the rage. On 1 January of that year Kenneth Tynan, then its most eminent drama critic, saw Bertolt Brecht's *Mutter Courage* in Paris, and portentously told his wife 'I am a Marxist'[2] – initiating a period of left-wing licence-to-bore almost as deadly as James Bond's licence-to-kill. The 1970s saw a brief vogue of denying the referentiality of language, when the jargon of *la nouvelle critique* was earnestly borrowed from Paris by advanced spirits, and novels for a time were called texts and denied social significance. There have been attacks from within, too, on the allegedly crippling tradition of British gentility in poetry and fiction, demands for a more Hegelian style in Anglo-Saxon philosophy, for French critical strategies, and for American fictional tolerance of the unmentionable. No forgotten outcast on a remote island ever had to put up with anything like this. The historian of the new Elizabethan age that began with the death of George VI in February 1952 would dutifully record the passing enthusiasms of the age along with its artistic victories. Britain is an island, but it is not culturally isolated. To be an island is to be exposed to the world, after all, not protected from it, and there is no keeping of foreign fashions out of London. I hope to have done justice to some of these shock-waves of taste, and without undue reverence. A sudden dedication to a foreign influence like Hegel or Derrida, brief but intense, is about the only thing there is that can cause the British to lose a sense of humour or a sense of proportion, and during the first London production of *Waiting for Godot* in 1955 I was reproached by strangers seated around me for laughing, though I still think it a funny play. The British seeker lost in the German metaphysical jungle, the homecomer from Paris dinner-parties armed with the latest idea, or what he hopes may pass for that, are abiding images for fun-making; and cultural insularity is a vice to be levelled against the British only by those who do not know them, though those who do sometimes have cause to wish it were true.

★   ★   ★

Decades have their spirits, their haunting obsessions, their characteristic aspirations; and though this book is governed not by chronology but by groups, by issues and by congeries of like minds, it is still possessed, always and inevitably, by a sense of evolving time. The years pass in parade like pageants in a dream. The 1940s were a decade split by the great peace that ended the last European war in May 1945, but it has its own domestic character – a character soon to be forgotten by succeeding decades, though in *The Girls of Slender Means* (1963) Muriel Spark aptly called it a time when 'all the nice people were poor'. It was idealistic and austere; its classic authors were George Orwell, who died in January 1950, and his friend Arthur Koestler; its spirit was resolutely decent and fiercely anti-totalitarian, its chosen mode a polemical prose that lost nothing of its edge by being cast, at times, into argumentative fictions like *Animal Farm* (1945), though its true forte was the article; and its best poet, Dylan Thomas, was manifestly a survivor from an earlier age. The 1950s saw the birth of the New Novel, more or less in the coronation year of 1953, with the first published fictions of Kingsley Amis, Iris Murdoch and William Golding: polemical still, but intent now on reviving a tradition of realism that had flourished first in eighteenth-century England, with Defoe and Fielding, and had faded somewhat in critical reputation in the inter-war years; and a revived realism spread rapidly into theatre, with John Osborne's *Look Back in Anger* (1956) and the first dramatic experiments of Harold Pinter. Next came the 1960s, perhaps the least Crusoe-like of the post-war decades, when a garnishing of foreign influences, like the fictional devices that decorate John Fowles's *The French Lieutenant's Woman* (1969), was sometimes felt to be a fashionable obligation, though it may be significant that Fowles's novel remains deeply rooted in a realistic tradition. The 1970s saw a return to a nationally more confident mood, with Amis fully established as a novelist and Philip Larkin as a poet, both of them roundly disdainful of foreign fads, and with the new drama of Tom Stoppard openly contemptuous of an intelligentsia once content to borrow its values from sources as alien and unassimilable as Lenin and James Joyce. And the 1980s have seen a determined rejection of imported fashions, the British novelist or dramatist speaking to his people in the confident expectation that the world at large, too, will insist on taking notice and asking for more.

All that represents an impressive reversal. The preceding age of English literature, after all, between the two world wars, had been notably un-British: its finest poets an American called T. S. Eliot and an Irishman called W. B. Yeats, its greatest novelists – Bloomsbury apart – James Joyce and a handful of Americans who, for the most part, had preferred to stay at home. By the

1930s the United States was coming to look like the rising star of the literary tradition, whether in poetry, drama, fiction or critical debate. Between the wars, in a word, English literature briefly ceased to be British, and there were those who imagined the change might easily be irreversible. Why, after all, should one small island in the North Atlantic continue forever to dominate a language it had once created, given that well over three-quarters of its native speakers now lived outside it? The doubt could be whispered in the 1930s, shouted in the 1940s and tacitly accepted as an established truth in the 1950s. Art follows wealth, it was said, as it did in the city-states of the Italian Renaissance; and it may continue to do so, even if the new patron happens now to be democratic and many-headed. Plutocracy inevitably governs the arts, it was suggested, as surely as it governs the terms of the trade. And to be rich, in the post-war world, could only mean dollar-rich.

That view has been little heard since the 1960s, when London reasserted a traditional suzerainty over theatre and literary publishing, and that so silently, and so naturally, that the reversion passed almost unnoticed. In that age English literature, like a prodigal, came home. This book, which might as easily have been entitled The Triumph of Realism, might equally have been subtitled The Return of the Native. Amis, Pinter and Osborne are London-born. J. R. R. Tolkien was born in South Africa, to be sure, Iris Murdoch in Dublin and Tom Stoppard in Czechoslovakia, but they settled into their lifelong home in childhood, and no one doubts they are British authors. By the late 1980s British publishing was issuing over 50 000 titles a year, more than 40 000 of them new titles, or well over a hundred (on average) for every working day. That is a lot of books. London, as it watched the decline of New York and Paris as theatrical capitals, maintained over fifty theatres, subsidised and commercial – of which most, on any week-day evening, were usually given over to legitimate theatre. British fiction, whether in original or in translation, often dominates sales across the world, and in a manner that might sometimes remind one, a little distantly, of the vast international triumphs of Walter Scott and Charles Dickens in their heyday. Economic growth since 1945 might be slow, and often was, manufactures sluggish and the national balance of payments too often in deficit; but in literature, by the 1960s, Britain was back. The whole world, by then, including the socialist world, wanted English. Students of literature, traditionally resentful as they often are to be told they might be engaged in anything severely useful, found they could sell their talents abroad as teachers, and had to tolerate the uncomfortably realistic view that the nation might recover through the teaching of English some small part of the wealth it had lost on technical adventures like building and running Concorde. In literature, if in little else, Britain was again a world power.

That return was uninfluenced by expatriates such as T. S. Eliot or Ezra Pound but profoundly influenced by the British past. If the native genius in literature is for comic realism, as I suspect, then the old-style Modernism of Eliot and Pound had little to say to it, or indeed to any attempt – serious or comic – to analyse a real world or to describe it. Modernism had been largely solemn. It was also hostile to realism and to any continuous attempt, by whatever means, to depict the real. That distinction marks out British popular literature and sub-literature as well as poems, plays and fiction. Ian Fleming's James Bond novels, from *Casino Royale* (1953) onwards, characteristically enough, are largely a comic creation; and though no one would dare call the Bond thrillers realistic, their strength was always at least as much in terms of observed social manners – dress, food, drink and forms of address – as in their innocently violent fantasies about sex and power in the age of the Cold War. The new comic tone was radical rather than left-wing, what is more, which may have been salutary to critics who glibly confuse social reform with social-ism. Amis's admiring study of Fleming, *The James Bond Dossier* (1965), acknowledged much of all that with a characteristic bluntness, and in 'a spiteful tangent' or side-swipe against Eliot and Modernism he remarked that 'a few mentions of (say) Nestlé's condensed milk, Woodbines, Spinks's plum-and-apple jam and Scotch-and-Apollinaris would have done *The Waste Land* a world of good', the lack of a socio-temporal context having left Eliot's poem 'just one more of the feature-less, flavourless lumps of cultural lumber it purports to be superior to'. This was a moment not for fairness but for plain speaking. Modernism, by then, had been around for a long time, and much of it looked ready to be stacked away into the attic. If Eliot had only managed to be funnier, some had come to feel, he would also have been more accurate. Life, after all, is funny.

Soap, whether radio or TV, suggests a similar national contrast. *Mrs Dale's Diary*, which ran for twenty-one years on BBC radio from 1948, was always gently laced with humour; its rural rival, *The Archers*, which began two years later, is a broadly similar amalgam of the playful and the sentimental; and between them, in a sub-literary sort of way, they illustrate the power of a revived realism in post-war Britain: quite different from the grand-opera histrionics of American TV soaps like *Dallas* or *Dynasty*, which are scarcely funny at all, at least in intention, and wildly unrealistic as images of how the rich in the United States really live. British radio works far closer to the texture of ordinary life than that, engaging as it does a deeper sympathy for a shared

world of ordinary experience and a total lack of awe. It is
accurate, in aspiration, and *The Archers* takes serious
trouble to get things right over the sowing and harvest-
ing of crops. It mixes humour and sentiment in a
characteristically insular way. When Grace Archer died
on BBC radio in 1955, some twenty million people, it is
said – perhaps half the adult nation – tuned in to hear,
though by the 1980s television had reduced the audience for radio soap to a mere three million. The comic,
the melodramatic and the sentimental easily mix anywhere; but on the eastern seaboard of the Atlantic it is
comedy, always comedy, that ultimately prevails. In
1954, for example, Galton and Simpson created *Hancock's Half Hour* on radio: satirical playlets about the pale
squalor of outer-suburban life that launched a series of
tiny exercises in comic realism to replace the music-hall
turns that had once dominated the BBC Light Programme: an earthy, irreverent spirit of realistic comedy
translated into visual terms in 1960, when Granada TV
started *Coronation Street* as a comic reflection, for mass
audiences, of back-street life in the urban North.

All that is a stirring of a native spirit, ultimately
uninnovative and well within the constraints of the
public will. 'We reflect society,' a director of soap once
remarked. 'We must not try to lead it.' To reflect society
can only mean comedy, in such a world, if a work is to
convince as any sort of mirror, and the preference of
other nations for melodrama and the bleeding heart has
nothing to do with the habitual temper of British life.
The grumbles of J. Alfred Prufrock in early Eliot are
endurable if they are meant to be ridiculous, but only
then; and sitting around on Margate sands, or anywhere
else, trying to connect nothing with nothing may be all
right for Harvard men abroad, but (as Eliot must already

have discovered when he wrote *The Waste Land*) it has nothing to do with the daily life of the Londoner.

Or with living anywhere. In a review of John Betjeman's verse-autobiography *Summoned by Bells* (1960), Philip Larkin remarked approvingly that Betjeman, in his triumphant lucidity, had managed to 'bypass the whole light industry of exegesis'; that Eliot's famous demand about the need of poets, in the present state of civilisation, to be difficult could only be an ingenious bit of intellectual job-creation, a Modernistic charter to make work for unemployed critics; and that the tradition of Kipling and A. E. Housman stood ready to hand for instant revival, ever eager to prove that poetry can still enjoy a reading public if only the poet is prepared to be simple, moving and memorable.[3] He was altogether right. Eliot's demand for difficulty, in retrospect, by now looks perverse as well as obscure. It is precisely in confused situations, after all, as travellers on the London Underground know, that people need clear maps, and the complexities of modern civilisation call not for literary difficulty but for literary clarity. Eliot's argument, never entirely convincing in its own age, had by the 1940s ceased to convince altogether. In 1940 Winston Churchill, as Prime Minister, told a crowded House of Commons stunned by the fall of France: 'My policy is victory'. By 1945 that policy had worked, and anyone who still wanted to get lost in mazes like Pound's *Cantos* was to be left to pursue his passion like a solitary vice.

By 1945 the real world was simply too urgent for prevarication. A hungry nation that rationed its scanty food-supplies till 1952 needed to be fed, its industries built or rebuilt, a health service kept open to all. The new Britain may have looked like a waste land by 1945, or at least a bomb site, especially in its inner cities. But it was surely natural for it to feel a flutter of impatience with a fading tradition of Edwardian Modernism that had once invited the educated reader to find metaphysical foundations to his faith before he could believe life meant anything or was worth living. The tasks of survival suddenly looked too urgent, and too grave, for the intellectual indulgences of Modernist metaphysics.

★   ★   ★

The new fiction of the age revived two contrasting types of English hero.

The first hero was gauche. He was an effortless survival of the 1930s, where fiction had abounded in well-meaning young men who had striven to Do the Right Thing and come to grief, at least till the last page of the story. P. G. Wodehouse's Bertie Wooster had been like that, in the Jeeves stories; so was Tony Last in Evelyn Waugh's *A Handful of Dust* (1934), a model country gentleman who loses child, wife, estate and ultimately England itself, marooned as surely as Crusoe in an inland jungle where he is forced to read Dickens's novels to an illiterate half-caste. Like *Brideshead Revisited* (1945), the novel is a fiercely funny tragedy: a paradox anticipated by *Little Dorrit*, however, which Waugh's luckless hero is left endlessly reading aloud to his captor, and a paradox utterly characteristic of a nation much given to finding laughter in despair. The hero of Waugh's *Sword of Honour* trilogy (1952–61), again, is virtuously gauche; so is Kingsley Amis's Lucky Jim in 1954, a comic hero usually as polite in aspiration as he is socially incompetent in practice; and so, it must be imagined, was the young Betjeman who, as he revealed in 'A Subaltern's Love-song' in *New Bats in Old Belfries* (1945), adored girls too strong for their fainting admirers, whether at love or tennis:

With carefullest carelessness, gaily you won,
I am weak from your loveliness, Joan Hunter Dunn.

The radio sketches that Galton and Simpson created for
Tony Hancock in the mid-1950s are a back-street version
of the same rueful joke: the hero, discomforted by every
encounter, gets it wrong when he is trying hardest to
get it right. The point is in no way irreverent or
anarchistic. In fact it is only because he is trying so hard
to get it right that he can be said to get it wrong at all,
and the gauche hero is above all the example of social
over-anxiety, like Betjeman's subaltern weak for love on
a Hampshire tennis-court: his palms moist at the first
handshake, one imagines, his over-careful manners a
veneer masking racking uncertainties, and an over-
developed sense of social duty enforcing its own inner
punishment. In life you cannot win, such works suggest, though you can find fun, even faith, in losing. The
luckless hero of Waugh's *Brideshead* ends tragically without wife, mistress or home; but he has followed Waugh
himself to Rome and its consoling faith, and at mass an
altar-flame burns for him in his soul 'farther in heart
than Acre or Jerusalem'. That was one man's choice. But
it started no religious fashions in post-war British
fiction, which is rootedly secular, its heroes as unbeliev-
ing of a world beyond the grave as they are insecure in
the only world they know.

The second hero, by contrast, is self-sufficient. That
looks incompatible with gaucherie, and perhaps is, but
it represents no more than the incompatibilities that
individuals daily enact in their own lives. British fiction
since 1945, whether novels or plays, abounds in heroes
who are benignly self-contained, and ashamed (if at all)
only of their own lack of any need for love. They are
emotionally strong: but can it be right, they wonder, to
be so strong? 'There isn't much loving in any of your

kindnesses, Jane,' the middle-aged hero of John Osborne's *Inadmissible Evidence* (1965) complains to his daughter in a long, unanswered diatribe against the younger generation – a new race of adolescents capable, for the first time, of subduing the earth around them and thinking nothing of it: 'not much kindness, not even cruelty, really, in any of you.' The spectacle of such self-sufficiency is vividly disturbing, especially in the young. The hero of Simon Gray's comedy *Otherwise Engaged* (1975), in similar fashion, only wants to be left alone to play his new recording of Wagner's *Parsifal*, but he is successively interrupted by neighbour, brother and wife, who succeed in disturbing him and fail only to interest him. Even the fact that his wife has a lover, is pregnant, and is uncertain who the father is, fails to hold his attention: he would rather listen to Wagner. Denis Cannan's *Dear Daddy* (1976), again, another successful stage comedy, tells of a virtuous middle-aged family man whose life is triumphantly self-organised down to its last petty details – exactly one-third of a bottle of wine at dinner every evening – until the comfortable domestic order he has created in his second marriage turns into an object of irrational despair to those around him; and when his first wife, ruined by alcohol, abruptly re-enters his world, he is forced to accept a share of deferred responsibility for the wreckage of her life. Iris Murdoch's novel *A Fairly Honourable Defeat* (1970) poses the far more terrible hypothesis of a being utterly without compassion who takes delight in wrecking the lives of others: his self-sufficient malignity seemingly motiveless until the last pages of the book, when a tattooed number is noticed on his arm, and a casual remark – 'I spent the war in Belsen' – forces the reader to think back through his destructive conduct as 'an instrument of justice' in destroying a happy marriage and endangering a harmonious relationship between two men. The novel argues in cold, unremitting fidelity to its own thesis that in life the evil may in the end go unpunished and live happily ever after; that the truly self-sufficient being, if he anywhere existed, would be ultimately inviolable, fearing neither reproach nor self-reproach; and that those who are strong enough to live without sympathy are forever beyond the reach of compassion or revenge. 'The food would probably be excellent,' the novel ends, as Julian the camp-survivor muses happily to himself in a sunlit Paris where he has settled, staring into a favourite restaurant in the Latin Quarter: 'He began to examine the menu. The sun was warm upon his back. Life was good.' A later Murdoch novel, *The Sea, the Sea* (1978), explores in the same unblinking fashion an aspect of human selfhood from another angle: its ageing hero, living cheerfully for himself and cooking dishes that hardly anyone else would want to eat, suddenly rediscovers a lost love, is deranged enough to kidnap her, fails to regain her love in captivity and is forced to accept, by the end, that his old self-sufficient life is all there is or can ever be. An earlier hero, in *The Black Prince* (1973), is a failed writer who creatively fulfils himself only in the enforced loneliness of a prison cell when he is convicted for a murder he has not committed. Solitude is always some sort of choice. But to be alone is not, in the end, to be lonely, and there are those who discover that in the end they need no one but themselves, and that solitude is more than enough.

That acceptance is perhaps more grim than smug, but as a comment on a modern post-industrial state it is, after all, quietly and sensibly realistic. Such heroes do not live like Robinson Crusoe, who survived on his island without tinned or frozen foods, refrigerator, air-conditioning or central heating. Britain after 1945 is full of people who live alone because they like it, or at

least because they like it better than any of the available
alternatives. They are the first tribe in human history of
wilful solitaries since the dissolution of the monasteries,
but their motives are in no way God-directed. Given
supermarkets and modern kitchen equipment, oneness
can easily be physically comfortable. Psychologically so,
too, given books, radio and television; and with the
right temperament, it can even be emotionally serene.
The temptation to stay alone at home and hear a
favourite programme rather than go to a party is after all
vividly real. Philip Larkin, a life-long bachelor, memorialised that dilemma in 'Vers de société' (1971), a short
poem where the conclusion, though finely balanced, is
only marginally in favour of going out for the evening.
'All solitude is selfish', the poet recalls having been told;
and no one now

> Believes the hermit with his gown and dish
> Talking to God (who's gone too); the big wish
> Is to have people nice to you,

and the motto nowadays, he reminds himself, is 'Virtue
is social'. But the ultimate truth, as the poem starkly
concludes, is that one goes out to counter the over-
balancing fear of being alone:

> . . . sitting by a lamp more often brings
> Not peace, but other things,

and the ageing solitary reluctantly lifts his pen to write
an acceptance-note. Even love, as he had explained five
years before in a poem briskly called 'Love' (1966), calls
for a lot of cheek: '. . . the blind persistence /To upset an
existence/Just for your own sake. 'Plainly a lot to ask of
anyone – far more than a momentary invasion of
privacy, which can be bad enough – and it is an

argumentative point that paradoxically makes self-sufficiency sound humble rather than arrogant.

A humble self-sufficiency – hard-earned, often enough, like Larkin's, and subject to sudden, spasmodic panics of loneliness or a fear of being thought insensitive – are the hallmark of many a post-war British hero, and no talk of anti-heroes can entirely rob it of its modicum of cautious praise. All heroes are in some measure anti-heroes, after all, if the term means that they are opposed to some antiquated sense of heroism that their creators are eager to question or discredit. 'The humble man,' as Iris Murdoch winningly remarked in *The Sovereignty of Good* (1970), 'because he sees himself as nothing, can see other things as they are', which sounds like a snug, confident view of humility, far removed from the self-lacerating anxieties about identity and self-image that mark out much of American fiction, or the radical scepticisms of Sartre and his disciples in post-war Paris. Those who, like Iris Murdoch, speak of a 'selfless attention' to others as a supreme mark of virtue – hard to achieve and harder still, as a duty, to discount – surely imply something like a deep security of inner being. And even after due allowance has been made for the undeniable fact, easily forgotten as it is, that literature is written by writers, and that writers are likely to be highly exceptional beings who actively prefer working alone, there is still something persuasively representative about the man in the play who would rather listen to a new recording of a favourite opera than to the problems of his neighbours and relatives. Other people may not be hell, as Sartre said, but they can undeniably be a nuisance. Hamlet the black prince knew that.

There is nothing much to be proud of, to be sure, in all this; and the self-sufficient hero, who knows it, is nothing of a boaster. One is fun, so they say. But to be all too sure of oneself – of who one is, of what one wants – might easily mean riding for a fall, and heroes in that style are prudently disinclined to flaunt their state of mind or to recommend it to others. The best hope is candidly to explain what one is, like Julian the camp-survivor and destroyer in *A Fairly Honourable Defeat*, and let others think what they may. But then the camp-survivor, by definition, is an extreme instance and a limiting case. More representatively there can be a sneaking hope that to explain is somehow to justify; and the novels, plays and poems that depict British self-sufficiency and its lapses often smack, like Larkin's poem 'Vers de société', of a sort of rueful mock-modesty: a determination to put a case for oneself as well as to record a mood. To prefer solitude with a book or a record-player is after all to have a case to answer – 'It's wrong to be by yourself' – though not, as some would say, an unanswerable case. Most books and music, one might reasonably reply, are better than most talk, and wives and lovers do fuss so. All this, in the end, is more than a question of style: it is a question of judgement and of taste, and ultimately of morality. There is an emerging argument here, if not for chastity, then at least for a prudent continence and a cool response to such favours, sexual or other, as the world may choose to offer.

That insistence on selfhood is characteristically national. In American fiction solitude, if in any way chosen, is commonly the sign of an unhinged mind like Saul Bellow's Herzog; and if not chosen, a matter of earnest compassion. 'It's wrong to be by yourself' is an American song, after all, and it is not on the whole a British sentiment. American poets can be so thunder-struck by the sheer oddity of being a poet in America at all that they often deny to the poet, in advance, any claim to represent a people or even a social class; and classic New York drama in this century, as in the plays of Eugene O'Neill and Arthur Miller, has concentrated painfully and insistently on the pre-eminence of family ties and the ineluctable need of everyone in that world to be loved, as they continuously imply, by their closest relatives. The great Latin literatures are implicitly social even when not explicitly that, and they seldom give credence to the view that a sane being in emotional health might reasonably prefer to be left to himself. The self-sufficient British hero, then, is nationally distinct. He simply does not need to be loved, apparently, whether by his relatives or anyone else; he does not even, at all reliably, want it. The narrator-hero of Kingsley Amis's *The Green Man* (1969), in most respects an ordinary chap, has to be persuaded by his wife even to drop in for family meals.

There is something impressively strong about all this, even if some would say that, like Diogenes telling Alexander to get out of his light, it looks a little like the strength of those who are content to be emotionally starved. Either way, a cheerful and faintly self-questioning sufficiency stands as the hallmark of the modern British literary mind, and it is without obvious sources at home or abroad. Victorian literature, after all, seldom if ever deals with the matter, and Wordsworth's bliss of solitude was an ideal aspiration of the poet, not a state he often claimed to have achieved. It is a mood resembling nothing, perhaps, in literature, on a long view, unless of Aristophanic comedy; but that must be coincidence. In the comedies of Aristophanes a hero is bothered and bludgeoned by a succession of intruders and enemies, much like the heroes of *Otherwise Engaged*, *Dear Daddy* or *The Sea, the Sea*. For those who love labels, then, modern British literature in that aspect might conveniently be called Aristophanic – provided, that is, it is well understood that its novelists and playwrights

cannot be assumed to have taken any attentive interest
in ancient Greek comedy, and that coincidence is all it is.

Coincidental or not, the Attic resemblance goes a little
further. Popular Athenian sentiment in ancient times
showed little sympathy for aliens, deviants or whingers,
and it could be rough on women as a species; and there
is a strong male smell of British-is-best among writers
newly emerged after 1945. All that is reactive. Modernists of the 1910s had been Latin-lovers, and often
enough (like Pound and Eliot) immigrants; Bloomsbury
was ardently francophile; and in the 1930s W. H. Auden
and his school, if only to show they were not Modernist
and not Bloomsbury, had haunted Hamburg and Berlin
and admired German communism. 1940 had put paid to
all that when, to echo a slogan, Britain and her Commonwealth stood alone, and the post-war cultural world
was in little doubt that British was best. Some of the
results of that mood were odd. With a fine disregard for
what was happening across the Channel, the Attlee
government convinced itself and others that the British
welfare state was unique in the world – to be deeply
startled in the 1950s by the news that many continental
neighbours had a more generous provision of social
welfare than the United Kingdom. The empire, at least
in Africa, was thought likely to outlast the century, not
least by socialist ministers; and it was imagined that the
Marshall Plan, paid off by the end of 1950, might
represent only a brief and passing reliance on the
economy of the United States. NATO, when it was
established in 1949, could be represented as the revival
of a war-time coalition rather than a realistic acceptance
that Britain could no longer defend herself. And the
European Community – even the Treaty of Rome which
had created a European Economic Community without
British participation in 1957 – could be dismissed by

Tories and Socialists alike, in its early years, as a dream and an illusion.

The underrating of Europe, the overrating of home, were two sides of the same coin. Kingsley Amis's third novel is symbolically called *I Like It Here* (1958). In his first, *Lucky Jim*, there had been an offensive character called Bertrand, a painter and a pacifist who preferred his name to be pronounced in the French manner: clearly a late derivative of Bloomsbury and a poseur of the worst water; and even if he were not a rival-in-love of the hero, that (one feels) would be all that needed to be said about him. John Wain's *The Contenders* (1958) ends with the most resonant and decorous of all English four-letter words, 'home', and the emphasis on a familiar term is the concluding point of the novel: 'In English I said "Home".' Philip Larkin, when asked by an interviewer if he ever read foreign poetry, archly replied '*Foreign* poetry?'; and there is a celebrated photo of the poet seated at the Scottish border, where the boundary-stone reads simply 'England'. Cities and regions can be even more confining. John Braine's first novel, *Room at the Top* (1957), was set in his native Yorkshire, and it contrived to make even London sound cosmopolitan and far away. And though Iris Murdoch occasionally sets a novel in Ireland – if that is the probable setting of *The Unicorn* (1963) – she commonly writes as someone who is a Londoner and proud of it. *A Word Child* (1975), indeed, is so specific in its references to places, and especially to places on the London Underground, that the narrator remarks he was once tempted to call his story the Inner Circle; and Martin Amis's *London Fields* (1989) is almost as detailed about Notting Hill as if it were a guide-book.

All this is a fresh literary image of home. Britain by the 1950s was no longer a waste land awaiting a sign or a messiah, as in Eliot, or a fading tapestry of social detail to recall earlier days as in Virginia Woolf. It may be scruffy, but it is where one belongs, and the only place one ever will belong: a world of pub-going rather than café-haunting, usually more self-examining than woundingly self-critical, and pleased (even grateful) to be alive, in a cautious sort of way. It is undefeated, after all – alone, apart from Russia, among the combatant nations of Europe – though it has heard the wings of defeat, and narrowly escaped its claws. It is tea and scones – and where else can you get a good cup of tea or a decent scone, or real beer, as the hero of one of C. S. Lewis's space-fictions reflects as he returns to earth and finds himself – miraculously and blissfully – in England and in a country village. Of course his first move is to go to a pub.

★   ★   ★

The principle of British-is-best was not without its challengers. If Britain means tea, scones and mild un-chilled beer, it also means moderate views, courtesy to strangers who ask the way in the street, and above all an avoidance of violence even as an idea. It was possible to dissent from all that, especially after a visit to New York. 'The concept of gentility', one young post-war critic complained,

> still reigns supreme. And gentility is a belief that life is always more or less orderly, people always more or less polite, their emotions and habits more or less decent and more or less controllable; that God, in short, is more or less good,[4]

and he quotes, as an instance, Larkin's famous early poem 'Church Going' (1954), where an unbeliever, once he is certain that 'there's nothing going on', enters a country church:

> Hatless, I take off
> My cycle-clips in awkward reverence.

The trouble with the British, the critic went on, and above all with British writers, is that they have no experience of invasion or concentration camps, and think politeness will always get you through. The argument is perhaps more tactical than serious, and it is a notable irony that the article was collected in 1968, in the very year when gentility, even in Britain, suffered a temporary eclipse. Talk about 'forging a new language' to describe new experiences forgets that an old language can sometimes express novelty better than any other; and the case fails to notice, too, that life depends on contrasts: that you cannot have informality without formality, bluntness without courtesy, indecorum without decorum. But tactical or not, the argument remains striking as a passing diagnosis, if unpersuasive as a programme. British literature is indeed polite. It is also, paradoxically, hard-hitting. On the opening page of Amis's first novel, Jim mentally decides on his own word when his professor uses another, deferentially pretending as an untenured lecturer to look amused at a weak professorial joke, and he promises himself to make another sort of face to himself when next alone. All this is a study in decorum, indeed – a decorum only narrowly maintained – but not in submission; and the demands of gentility do not inhibit the novelist when he writes. They add spice to the mixture. As for the artistic effects of invasion and concentration camps, that can only prompt the awkward question whether the ensuing creativity of occupied Europe ever justified the price that was enforced and paid.

★   ★   ★

British literature since 1945 has not proved a coterie literature, on the whole, though it has occasionally grouped itself, at least notionally, into informal sets. That, too, may have been reactive to Modernism and Bloomsbury, which were certainly coteries, though in a land traditionally sceptical of manifestoes and cynical about self-advertisement it may as easily have been the reassertion of an ancient mistrust. The Modernists had enjoyed a brief life as a London group after Pound settled there for a dozen years in 1908; Bloomsbury was already one, first in Cambridge and later in London and Sussex, sharing not just a range of assumptions and convictions but an intimate web of social and amorous relations. In the 1930s Auden & Co. had been another; with Auden himself, as early as his undergraduate days at Oxford in the late 1920s, confidently apportioning literary roles to Isherwood, Spender and himself.

All this looks continental, above all French, and the post-war world was to prove less tidy and less lucid. Dylan Thomas was a cult-poet, indeed; but in Britain, at least, his poetic followers achieved little, and even before his death in New York in 1953 his influence was greater in America than at home. Koestler and Orwell met and became friends during the war, but it takes more than two to make a coterie, and in conversation Koestler denied having taught Orwell anything important about communism: it was a meeting, not always entirely harmonious, of like minds. As for the Movement, or the Angry Young Men of the 1950s, the intellectual and popular press were not wrong to believe that a new race of novelists (and others) had appeared in the first months of the new reign, soon after the death of George VI; but the name Movement coined by a *Spectator* journalist in 1954 never seemed likely to fit for long, or Angry Young Men either; they never met as a group, though they were (at least for the most part) acquainted. A *Zeitgeist* is all the more convincingly that, it may be argued, if it reveals itself simultaneously and without conspiracy or foreknowledge, but some of the cards in this pack look pretty wild. Colin Wilson's *The Outsider*, for example, which by a glorious coincidence appeared in May 1956 – the very month of the appearance of John Osborne's first performed play *Look Back in Anger* – was a bookish, self-educated exegesis of a fat clutch of heady topics including violence and mysticism, all untidily carved out of a huge, unfinished novel about Jack the Ripper. The book and the play were inevitably reviewed together, and the play is undoubtedly an explosion of anger by a young dramatist obsessed by a fierce personal conviction that he has been socially slighted. Colin Wilson, however, may have been justified in remarking years later that he has never been angry about anything,[5] and Kingsley Amis has grown angry by growing conservative and old. Radicals need not be angry at all, and *Lucky Jim* is too confident a book, surely, to be described in that way. Its keynote is not anger but scorn.

There were, none the less, one or two groups in post-war Britain that merit the name of coterie, if the word implies a repeated or regular gathering of like-minded writers in the same room. The Inklings, centred on war-time and post-war Oxford, were such a group: they were dedicated to a revival of Christianity and to literary story-telling, and they engendered the novels and polemics of C. S. Lewis and Tolkien's huge romance *The Lord of the Rings* (1954–5). That is a rare instance, in British literary annals, of a band of brothers achieving in broad terms, for a time, what it had once set out to do. Other groups are less coherent. Amis in a radio interview has spoken of his war-time friendship at Oxford with Philip Larkin as if it had succeeded only in inverted terms. 'We had it all shared out,' he remarked of his meeting with Larkin in April 1941. 'I was to be the poet, he the novelist. Funny how it turned out', meaning that it turned out the other way.[6] Plainly Britain is not France. But even in Britain literary friendships, often formed as early as school or university, can start a periodical, write a manifesto and continue spasmodically through life to inform a style and promote a habit of mind. People often write novels because they know a novelist, poems because they know a poet, plays because they know a playwright. Such alliances tend to be as fleeting as the chance encounters and re-encounters of fictional characters in Anthony Powell's *A Dance to the Music of Time* (1951–75); and the conversation of young friends, as potent in all likelihood as any literary influence there is, is largely beyond the reach of the historian, even the contemporary historian, except as guesswork. When Amis visited his friend Larkin at Leicester University College after the war, fresh from the army, he sat in a chair in the senior common room, listened to the academic gossip, sniffed the air and said: 'Yes, I could stand this' – to become a lecturer in Swansea. No wonder, then, if *Lucky Jim*, dedicated though it is to Larkin, was thought to be about life in Swansea University College, which it never was.

The creative mind is moved at least as much by those it knows as by what it reads, but the matter is largely obscure and often simply undiscoverable. If, then, in the pages that follow, I group authors by friendship, acquaintance and sheer fellow-feeling, even though strangers or near-strangers, this is a device adopted for clarity and convenience, and little more.

2

Orwell/Waugh

Parallel lines, it is said, never meet. The literary lives of Evelyn Waugh and George Orwell ran parallel through the 1930s and 1940s, and they met only once – in 1949 – the meeting proving wholly unmemorable, as it happens, for its conversation. The dogmatic gap between them still looks unbridgeable: Right against Left, Christian against secular, ancient against modern. They had entered the Second World War opposed in attitude, and emerged little changed.

So it must have seemed even to them. Born in 1903, a year before Graham Greene, they met only when Orwell was dying; and only a few letters are known to have passed between them, all composed in polite terms, as if to strangers. For some twenty years they had taken opposite sides, reliably and predictably, on all the resounding issues of religion and state. And yet, as if to contest all that, there is evidence that each read the other with respect, even avidity, occasionally sending copies of recent books as if eager for comment and commendation.

Their marriage of mind barely peeps above the surface of surviving documents, though it is plain enough in the two masterpieces they produced in 1945, *Brideshead Revisited* and *Animal Farm*. Respect was always guarded. Some months before his early death in January 1950, Orwell had agreed to write an article on Waugh for an American journal. Drafted in March 1949, the article never emerged beyond a few notes, mainly about *Brideshead* itself, though the task led him to reread all Waugh's early works, including his biographies, and it was evidently one the dying man approached with enthusiasm. The notes are sadly predictable, however, in their dogmatism. Waugh was a good writer ruined, Orwell concluded, by superstition: 'about as good a novelist as one can be ... while holding untenable opinions', and the death of Lord Marchmain at the end of *Brideshead* predictably repelled him, when an apparently unregenerate peer silently makes the sign of the cross and the two lovers, though divorced, realise in a religious ecstasy that they can never marry. 'The veneer is bound to crack, sooner or later,' Orwell acidly remarks. 'One cannot really be Catholic and grown up.'[1]

That was the secular side. For the other, Waugh had already praised Orwell's *Critical Essays* (1946) in somewhat distant terms, as representing 'at its best' the hated humanism of the Common Man.[2] That Rooseveltian tag was much in the air as war ended, on both sides of the Atlantic, and it was a populist view for which Waugh, whose aspirations were unfailingly patrician, never hesitated to disguise his profound distaste. 'I do not presume to counsel my sovereign on the choice of her advisers,' he once grandly told a journalist who had rashly asked him how he was going to vote in a parliamentary election. But it is notable that his review of Orwell is not hostile or ungenerous. He aptly compares him to Edmund Wilson, as a stylist, and one feels Orwell's formula could easily have been returned: about as good a writer as one can be while holding untenable opinions. Waugh especially admired Orwell's pioneering essay on the social implications of the vulgar seaside postcard, 'The Art of Donald McGill' (1941); but he lamented his rooted incapacity to esteem or even entertain any hint of religious sentiment – all the more striking and regrettable, he argues, in one plainly en-

dowed with 'an unusually high moral sense and respect
for truth and justice'.

The contrast looks complete. But it may still be worth
striving to see the Right-Left medal of that contentious
era as a whole, its opposite sides complementary as well
as antagonistic. All over the Western world an intelligentsia had recently been at war with itself: the
screaming-point being reached and passed in 1935–6,
with Mussolini's violent seizure of Ethiopia and the
outbreak of civil war in Spain. Waugh and Orwell took
opposite sides on Ethiopia and Spain; but not on Hitler,
for whom Waugh never showed a particle of sympathy,
and his anti-Hitlerism was even to become something
like a practical ideal for Orwell. 'Why can't someone on
the Left ever do something like that?' he remarked
admiringly to Anthony Powell in 1941, when he heard
Waugh had joined a commando unit.[3] Beneath their
opposition there was often an undercurrent of admiration and fellow-feeling. 'Unlike a lot of people, I thought
Brideshead Revisited was very good,' Orwell remarked in
a letter in July 1948, 'in spite of hideous faults on the
surface.'[4] Waugh might have agreed even with the
complaint about surface faults, which he was shortly to
concede in a new preface and expunge by revision. He
had already admired *Animal Farm* which, as he tells in
his diary (31 August 1945), he read promptly on its first
appearance to spite his cousin Claud Cockburn, who as
a loyal Communist Party man had warned him against
reading Trotskyite literature. (Counter-suggestibility
was something else Waugh and Orwell had in common.) The book evidently proved a pleasure rather than
a duty, part of the pleasure being political; and there is
an added spice to his enjoyment of Orwell's anti-
Stalinist fable that needs to be pondered.

The copy of *Animal Farm* Waugh read in the summer

of 1945 to spite his communist cousin had been sent to him by Orwell himself, whom he had never met. In fact Waugh had just written to him as a stranger to thank him for his 'ingenious and delightful allegory' – his gratitude all the warmer because, as he flatteringly remarks, he had tried to buy a copy and found it sold out. Authors like to be told such things. A second letter is similarly formal; and only the third – 'dear Orwell – Blair? – which do you prefer?' breaks any ice, hesitating between a famous pseudonym and Orwell's real name of Eric Blair. Once again he has to thank him for a new book, this time *Nineteen Eighty-Four* (1949); but now he sounds cool. It had 'failed to make my flesh creep', he reports guardedly, in a phrase he was to repeat years later about it in his life of Ronald Knox (1959), and failed because it had denied the existence of the soul and omitted all mention of the Church. And that, Waugh protests, is simply incredible. However bad things might prove to be decades hence, in 1984, they could not be so bad that religious feeling would simply have died out; and he promises to visit Orwell in his illness, which he did. Nothing memorable happened at their only meeting, in a Gloucestershire sanatorium, though Malcolm Muggeridge once remarked that he would have loved to see and hear them together, and it is still open to anyone to write an imaginary conversation of the event. As Muggeridge says, it must have been visually interesting, at least, with Waugh's 'country-gentleman's outfit and Orwell's proletarian one, both straight out of back numbers of *Punch*'.[5]

★   ★   ★

If nothing else, their congeniality was stylistic. The debonair style they both preferred for handling issues grave or grim was part of an improbable legacy from

P. G. Wodehouse, whose inter-war writings they had both admired from boyhood on. In fact they exchanged hints for Orwell's own essay on Wodehouse (1945); and years after Orwell's death, Waugh was to praise him in a broadcast for having generously helped to save Wode-house from the undeserved public disgrace of prosecu-tion as a war-time Nazi collaborator.[6] The common secret of their fiction, in brief, was to put Wodehouse's gaiety to a serious purpose, and it was a secret they were happy as strangers to share. Hard to remember, between readings, that *Brideshead* and *Nineteen Eighty-Four* are funny books: one recalls so vividly the gravity of their themes, so little the gaiety of their prose, that a rereading can easily surprise.

Both, what is more, were masters of a species of invective at once tough and suave. This is a style of abuse that has excited some natural envy among profes-sional satirists. 'Pow, and you're down,' Norman Mailer once remarked admiringly of Orwell's prose, in a tele-vised interview, imitating with a boxer's punch the flash of a fist. That pow is a gift Waugh and Orwell shared. It is there when Orwell calls the Left 'Bolshevik commis-sars, half gangster, half gramophone, escaped quakers, vegetarian cranks and back-room Labour Party crawl-ers', or when he dismisses the Marxist dialectic as an argumentative pea-and-thimble trick; there again when Waugh reviews Stephen Spender's flatulent autobiogra-phy *World within World* (1951):

> To see him fumbling with our rich and delicate language is to experience all the horror of seeing a Sèvres vase in the hands of a chimpanzee.[7]

Such masters of the merciless put-down must have studied each other's writings through the long intellec-tual civil wars of the 1930s and after with a mounting respect that no dogmatic divide could dim. If not soul-mates, they were always style-mates; and the fierce trenchancy that characterises literary life at its liveliest, in a polemical age, never found finer exponents. 'British intellectual knife-throwing' and American admirer once appreciatively called it, as one accustomed to the blander or blunter literary world of the United States. It is sad that Orwell should have been bedridden and dying when he met Waugh, for the first and last time. They might have enjoyed each other.

Beyond style there are profounder kinships. Orwell's mind-transforming discovery in 1937, in Barcelona – that political extremes meet and that fascism and communism are much alike – is one Waugh had already made, and the charge that he was ever knowingly indulgent to fascism is unjustified. His views on Ethiopia and Spain in 1935–6 had been misguided, many would say; but it is a question whether fascism, in his own understanding of the matter, ever entered into it, though Christianity decidedly did. His irreverent view of black states had already been comically revealed in *Black Mischief* (1932); and as a convert to Rome in 1930 he watched in 1936, and without regret, the overthrow of a Spanish Republic violently intolerant of a Church he loved. In any case he had the deepest contempt, first to last, for the facile conceptualising that often passes for advanced thought, rather like Orwell's contempt for W. H. Auden's partisan poem 'Spain' (1937):

The conscious acceptance of guilt in the necessary
murder

of which Orwell had derisively remarked in 'Inside the Whale' (1940) that it could only have been written by an innocent for whom murder is at most a word. Orwell's jibes at Auden's emigration to New York in January

1939, too, with Christopher Isherwood, were to be echoed shortly after by Waugh in *Put Out More Flags* (1942), which he composed on a troopship. He called Isherwood Parsnip in that novel because of his face, presumably, and Auden was Pimpernel because he had saved Thomas Mann's daughter from the Gestapo by contracting a Platonic marriage. Running away from a national crisis, at all events, was conduct that Waugh and Orwell saw as one.

The large dogmatic difference remains. But it may not be too late to suggest that Waugh's reputation for right-wingery – a reputation swallowed by Orwell and many since – has been mildly overdone. His mind was too surprising, as Orwell's was, to be so easily labelled. In *A Tourist in Africa* (1960), for example, a travel book composed long before hostility to apartheid was widely fashionable, Waugh bluntly called it 'racial insanity', on the grounds that it 'fantastically choose[s] pigmentation as a determining factor'. Black/white, he argued, is a 'preposterous frontier', being grossly over-simple, and the world needs far more discriminations than simple divisions between negro and white or Gentile and Jew. Snobbery, as he knew, if subtly and intelligently interpreted, is vastly different from racialism, and one reason why Waugh was not a racialist is that he was so inveterately and intricately a snob, and devotedly believed in shadings and gradings. 'Stable and fruitful societies have always been elaborately graded', he wrote, and the mistake of apartheid was to make a single decisive distinction on one ground – skin-colour – and then to elevate into a rigid legal system what rightly belongs to a world of personal inclination. In sum, Waugh was conservatively anti-modern rather than right-wing, and racialism (as he rightly saw) was 'rather modern' – meaning Victorian, unlicensed by traditional religion and unknown to the universal Church.

Orwell would not have put it like that. But his mature convictions were the effect of a long organised retreat from the simple dualities of youthful Marxism – capitalism against socialism, bourgeois against prole – and the first of his books ever to see print, *Down and Out in Paris and London* (1933), had been emphatic that Marxist analysis fails to correspond to observed experience, the gradations insisted on by the kitchen-staff of a Parisian hotel or the destitute of an English doss-house being there because the poor want them to be there and not by compulsion. Hierarchy is not imposed from above, then, but demanded from below: a fact that many theorists of class-conflict are powerless to understand and incompetent, at times, even to remark.

It is notable, what is more, that the contempt of Orwell and Waugh for simplistic systems like apartheid and communism – black or prole versus white or bourgeois – has nothing, in the end, to do with egalitarianism. Neither of them believed that mankind was equal, or could ever be so, or would ever seriously wish to be so. All systems based on the ideal of equality break down in action: that is a point that might be expected of Waugh, but it is Orwell who makes it the more forcefully: 'Some animals are more equal than others', as the pigs decree in *Animal Farm*, symbolising the easy self-justifications of Leninists in taking and keeping power. The folly of Moscow and Pretoria, both would have agreed, lies in their common determination to institutionalise differences where nature itself offers only subtleties and complexities. Marxism and racialism are 'rather modern', as Waugh would have put it, mindful that the medieval schoolmen and Renaissance Jesuits he idolised would have seen no merit in either of them. They are bookish, theoretical, and what Orwell in 'Inside the Whale' once perceptively called 'largely based on a sense of personal immunity'. (Who, after all, ever thinks of *himself* as a bourgeois?) Perhaps all that makes it easier to understand why Orwell was so anxious that Waugh should read his books: anxious enough to send him copies, though to a stranger.

★   ★   ★

As novelists, however, Orwell and Waugh evolve not towards each other but, technically speaking, in opposite directions. Waugh's novels grow towards realism as he ages, that is to say, after 1945, and Orwell's away from it.

Orwell, unlike Waugh, was never a natural master of narrative, and his uncertain career in fiction had begun, after much trial and error, with *Burmese Days* (1934), where he had exploited his youthful experiences in the Burma police. It was only in the last six or seven years of his life that he discovered that his talents lay elsewhere: in polemics, above all, and in what Waugh in his letter of thanks for *Animal Farm* had called ingenious and delightful allegory. Strictly speaking Orwell's book is perhaps less an allegory than a *conte philosophique* like Voltaire's *Candide* or Samuel Johnson's *Rasselas*; Swift's *Gulliver's Travels* is not far off here either, as a source, and it is certain that Orwell profoundly admired Swift, as Waugh admired Voltaire. English fiction in 1945 was already beginning to return to its eighteenth-century roots – a return confirmed soon after by Kingsley Amis, John Wain and Iris Murdoch, where the realism of Defoe and Fielding was to be self-consciously revived. Orwell and Waugh, older by a generation, belonged to an earlier and a sparer tradition. Characters are cut-outs, mental events are banned as if the Bloomsbury tradition needed to be ruthlessly exorcised, and names like Miles Malpractice in *Vile Bodies* explain characters in boldly extra-realistic ways, much as they might have done in

Bunyan's *Pilgrim's Progress*. This is a daring technical return. Waugh had seen the opportunities of the *conte* almost twenty years earlier than Orwell; but he had exhausted his interest before war broke out in 1939, so that *Brideshead* and the *Sword of Honour* trilogy are firmly planted in a revived realistic tradition. Orwell saw the point of technical reaction rather belatedly, but the example must have encouraged him. In a war-time article on Smollett he remarked that several writers had recently tried to 'revive the picaresque tradition', instancing Waugh and Aldous Huxley – adding that the experiment had not been entirely happy, if only because they had betrayed a sense of strain in an effort to be shocking.[8] The term *picaresque* is used pretty loosely here, no doubt, as it often is, to mean something like episodic and comically adventurous. That fits Waugh's 1930s fiction well enough, and in an age that had been reading Proust, Joyce and Virginia Woolf it must all have looked startlingly diagrammatic and technically reactionary: a reactionary politics aptly matched by a technical reaction.

Why did British fiction so suddenly revive the *conte philosophique* in the years around the war's ending, along with its fierce, diagrammatic crudities of tone and substance?

Anthony Powell, who once encouraged Waugh to write his first full-length book – a biography of Rossetti (1928) – has suggested that Waugh revived simplicity because he was himself simple:

> He saw human beings not as a mass of contradictions but as a particular sort of person – a great nobleman or a poor scholar or a spotty-faced announcer from the BBC. That was all they were, and they had to go through life like that.[9]

But that is talent speaking of genius, and it overlooks
the protective colouring by which genius can seek to
mask its own sensitivities. 'He was an extraordinarily
uncomplicated man,' Powell adds, 'who saw life in very
simple terms.' Simplicity, however – at least the sort that
scores in argument or fiction – can be a highly achieved
state of mind, 'costing not less than everything', and
only highly complex beings arrive at it at all, or need to
seek it out. Perceiving that fascism and communism
were more like each other, by 1945, than either was like
the civilisation of the West is an instance of achieved
simplicity, and one that Waugh and Orwell indepen-
dently shared. In his autobiography *A Little Learning*
(1964) Waugh was to observe that at the age of sixteen
he noticed that his publisher father, 'whom I had grown
up to accept with complete simplicity', was in fact a
highly gifted actor in everything he did. Orwell's simplicity was much like that parent-figure: it can suddenly
look more complicated, and more assumed, than one
had at first supposed. He once remarked that good
prose is like a window-pane, meaning that you ought to
be able to see through it without seeing it; and anyone
who has ever tried to write prose like that, or to see
human creatures in life or fiction like Waugh's early
fictional characters, will know how much clutter of
mind and words needs first to be cleared away. Windows have to be cleaned often if they are to be kept
clean, and literary clarity, too, is always likely to be an
effect of long labour. If Waugh and Orwell did not
exactly despise the complexities of Modernism, Joyce-
style or Eliot-style, at least they recognised, and early,
that such complexities were not for their times and not
for them. An urgent age needed something sharper and
cleaner than that. Orwell once modestly remarked that
Joyce's *Ulysses* made him feel like a eunuch taking
singing lessons, and Waugh's artist-hero in *Brideshead*

briskly calls modern art bosh. Stupid people have thought such things about Joyce, to be sure, and about the school of Picasso. But that does not mean that all who have thought such things are stupid.

*   *   *

Seeing the convergence of communism and fascism took a kind of intelligence that Joyce and Eliot did not have, and one they might not much have respected.

That convergence is the concluding point of *Animal Farm*, which ends on a sudden vision of a resemblance, even an identity, between the warring representatives of two dictatorial orders: '. . . already it was impossible to say which was which'. By a supreme irony Waugh was to echo the point, coincidentally, in the very letter to Nancy Mitford that bore the tidings of Orwell's premature death. That was in January 1950, when Europe was still reeling from the revelations of the Nazi death-camps, opened less than five years before, and the voluminous confirmations of the Nuremberg trials of what war-criminals had done there. Waugh knew as well as Orwell that Nazism was not a conservative idea but a false and perverted progressive idea – an idealism gone wrong. 'Gas chambers were not a Nazi invention,' he told her. 'All "Progressives" . . . believed in them, and called it Euthanasia', characteristically exaggerating a sensible point with 'all'. Half a century before, it is true, H. G. Wells and Havelock Ellis had proclaimed that socialism would require the extermination of the unfit by the state; and soon after, Bernard Shaw had urged scientists to devise painless methods of killing, since the new society would tolerate only workers, and the doctrine of the sanctity of human life, like all doctrines of sanctity, was antiquated claptrap. To adapt Orwell's last sentence, it is almost impossible to say which was which, so profound and intimate are the links that bind the intellectual socialism of the early twentieth century to the National Socialism that sought confidently in the 1930s to replace it. A pity Orwell and Waugh found no chance to discuss such weighty questions when they met, for the first and last time, in 1949. On modern totalitarianism there is a kinship of interest between them deeper than the ocean and higher than the stars.

★   ★   ★

Such, too, was the theme that intensified in their fiction towards middle age, which may be called the agony of a lost Eden.

The idea, which smacks of Milton, was potent in the age. Edwin Muir's *One Foot in Eden* (1956) is a last collection of poems by an Orkney poet whose passion for ancient myth was an expression of something deeper still – a profound distrust of the urban, the rootless and the industrial – and he repeatedly glimpsed, with a painful sense of loss, a paradise beyond grey modernity:

> Oh here the hot heart petrifies
> And the round earth to rock is grown
> In the winter of our eyes;
> Heart and earth a single stone.
> Until the stony barrier break
> Grief and joy no more shall wake,

as he ended 'Song for a hypothetical age', in near-despair. Muir was to die soon after, in 1959, and it is a poem that poses in brief the same paradox as Milton's epic. How, after all, can one miss something one has never known? Waugh and Orwell, like Muir, knew that one can. Eden is always somewhere else, or someone else's – or else it is snatched away after only a moment, at most, or only distantly seen, felt or known. Paradise is lost, so to speak, almost before it is found, and it is never possessed and savoured. Winston Smith, Orwell's hero in *Nineteen Eighty-Four*, dimly knows there was once a free England before the Party seized total power, and he wanders off alone into the London slums to find memories of it. *Brideshead*, too, is an exercise in passionate nostalgia, and of a kind that has sometimes been held to be embarrassing, since it celebrates the dying life of a great country house, though such critical embarrassments may be more ritual than real. True to form, Orwell in his notes on Waugh disapprovingly named snobbery and Catholicism as the two driving forces of the novel, and as a secular radical he must have felt obliged to reprobate the one as much as the other. Kingsley Amis, similarly, once remarked on television how much he disapproved of the book – 'Nobs' appeal,' he remarked crushingly, 'the appeal of nobs,' though he generously added that he often reread it. There is plainly a surprising depth of sympathy here between Waugh and the secular, radical mind, and one somehow richer and deeper than either religion or politics: a fellow-feeling about a paradise forever beyond reach.

What is that lost Eden? Orwell in his notes offers only the ghost of an answer when he remarks that Waugh's loyalty was to a form of society no longer viable, 'of which he must be aware'. Waugh is indeed aware of it, and that is the piercing tragedy at the heart of *Brideshead*. More than that, and far worse, he is aware that he could not have it for himself even if it did exist. Difficult, at this distance, to shut out of mind photographs of Waugh in his later years in his modest country house, forever trying to look like a country gentleman and forever (as a friend once remarked) looking like a bookie. That was the notoriously comic side of his social failure. But in *Brideshead* the point runs sharper and deeper. As the novel amply shows, those who want can't have and – what only makes it harder to bear – those who have don't want. The hero's Oxford friend, Lord Sebastian, has the magnificent baroque pile of Brideshead for his ancestral home, and he detests it. 'It's where my family live,' he says distantly, and slowly drinks himself to death. Charles Ryder, whom he introduces first to the enchanted world of the great English house and then to Venice, would give all he ever had, and far more, to live in such high ceremonial heavens – 'I was drowning in honey, stingless' – and is forever shut out. The novel, in that aspect, is romantic auto-biography. As a boy Waugh had longed to go to Eton, which might have made a radical of him and where he might have met Orwell, and did not; his first aristocratic wife left him after a year, and for an Etonian; and his sojourns in a great Elizabethan house in Worcestershire as a young man, the guest of a friend, allowed him to glimpse a world of moats, battlements and rolling parkland from which in spirit he never awoke. 'The smiling meadows of Worcestershire and the noble line of the Malvern hills that I love so dearly', he wrote to a member of that titled family from the swamplands of British Guiana in January 1933, missing and yearning for a home he knew could never be his.

In much of his fiction, early and late, Waugh turns from comedy to the haunting thought of a lost Eden; and in a nation that had once been the first industrial civilisation that can only mean a pastoral world. He wrote his own novels like that, and read the novels of others like that. The best part of *Nineteen Eighty-Four*, he told Orwell in his letter of July 1949, announcing his visit, was 'the delicious conversation in the pub when Winston tries to pump the old man for memories of pre-revolutionary days', and one might easily have

guessed that Waugh would think that episode the best.
It is about a paradise one cannot have.

Orwell's point here was perhaps richer than Waugh's,
in the end, and richer simply because he was Orwell.
Everyone, after all, knows that conservatives are in love
with the past: everyone expects it. It took an Orwell to
see that radicals need it too, and need it more than
others. 'He who controls the past controls the future' is
the message of his last utopia: a sense of history is
ultimately power, since a people is guided and governed by a collective sense of what it means to itself and
to the world, and history gives it that sense, and only
history. When Winston Smith and O'Brien pledge themselves to a revolution against dictatorship, the toast is
not to the future but to the past which, as O'Brien puts it
with mock gravity, is 'more important'. Marxism, after
all, was a theory of history, and a radical one. To
understand the world one is in is to understand where it
came from, and how it came; and it is only because it is
understood, or thought to be, that one can aspire to
change it. That is why radicals need the past not just as
much as conservatives but more than they.

At the age of twenty Evelyn Waugh wrote a story for
Harold Acton called 'Anthony, Who Sought the Things
That Were Lost'. Winston Smith seeks such things in
Orwell's last book when he enters the slums of London
to find someone old enough to remember an England he
himself had never known. At the end of *Brideshead*, too,
Waugh's hero is defeated in a similar search, though he
is allowed consolation. Waugh perceived a resemblance
between the two books himself, and in his letter to
Orwell on *Nineteen Eighty-Four* he reproached him in a
jibe as potent as any he ever made to friend or enemy:
'Men who love a crucified God need never think of
torture as all-powerful.' That, after all, at the end of
Orwell's book, is just what Winston Smith has been

forced to think when, subjected to torment of mind and body, 'he loved Big Brother'. Strange, perhaps, that the conservative should be more optimistic than the radical, but it is notable that *Brideshead* does not end in Orwellian despair. Its hero has lost wife, mistress and even the cause he fights in, since the war against dictatorship lost most of its point for Waugh on a day in June 1941 when Hitler invaded Russia. Even the great country house his hero had once hopelessly loved, as an outsider, has been ruined by military occupation; and the army that has ruined it, as he bitterly recognises, is his own. 'I have been here before' is his echoing cry as, in the deprivations of war and middle age, he remembers his time there with Sebastian twenty years before: two youths in love, one clutching at a toy to recall the lost innocence of a child.

And so Charles Ryder, now a convert, goes to mass, and in the family chapel he had once in agnostic youth admired only as a work of art in a strange and alien style. To borrow Sebastian's words, he has buried something there, and wants to find it. 'I should like to bury something precious in every place where I've been happy,' Sebastian had once told him, after wine and strawberries on a summer hilltop, 'and then, when I was old and ugly and miserable, I could come back and dig it up and remember.' More fortunate than Orwell's hero, Charles is back to dig it up. He has lost everything and gained a faith, and he knows that in the chapel a flame burns for him. No wonder a fellow-officer remarks how cheerful he looks, when he comes back. For he has discovered that the task of one's mature years is to forgive the follies of youth: for having loved too much, above all, and too often, and too soon.

3

Christian Revival: Tolkien and Lewis

Christianity, someone once said, is the eternal after-thought of history.

The dictum echoes a mood wider than post-war Britain, where the moment of Christian revival among the lettered was brief and limited in scope. It was none the less a moment of grave concern to unbelievers of any reliable militancy. William Empson, a lifelong and dedicated atheist, returned from the Far East in 1952 expecting to find little more demolition-work on religion needing to be done, at least among the lettered, and was horrified to discover that the devout spirit of T. S. Eliot, in his absence, had spawned a host of converts in the critical world. The popular success of C. S. Lewis's broadcasts, published in 1942 as *The Screwtape Letters*, aroused at least as much indignation as their provocation had plainly sought and deserved, being composed in radical irony out of the mouth of a Devil instructing an acolyte how to spread scepticism and moral confusion through the modern world. Believing in God was bad enough, it was felt: believing in the Devil, which few enough modern clergymen were known to do, was far worse. To coin a phrase, Lewis's war-time broadcasts on behalf of God put a pigeon among the cats. In *The Emperor's Clothes* (1953) Kathleen Nott called the Christian revivalism of Eliot, Lewis and others no better than a revived superstition; and in a scathing attack on contemporary dogmatics and the anti-progressive views of literary Modernism she remarked, in tones of ultimate scorn, that Lewis's interest in the Devil had plumbed unusual depths.

Religious conviction, in that age, and still more religious observance, were seen as naturally conservative; and the Christian revival of the 1940s was openly regressive, anxious above all that the world might be changing too fast and too far. The school of Tolkien, if one may so describe it, was an attempt to throw on the brakes: to rediscover a national and personal selfhood by discovering the roots of faith. In the years between the wars G. K. Chesterton and Evelyn Waugh had been converts to Rome. The Inklings, as they liked to call themselves, were more commonly Anglican, but their views were blatantly traditional and unashamedly patriotic and backward-looking. J. R. R. Tolkien (1892–1973), a Catholic by upbringing, wrote in praise of the remembered virtues of the British Tommy in the trenches during the First World War, and the enormous and highly improbable success of *The Lord of the Rings* (1954–5), for all that it began as a cult in the United States rather than at home, struck a chord that was ultimately insular, tribal and boldly British. Where Modernists like Pound and Eliot had been intruders into island life, the new school of Christian apologists, in every sense that matters, were British bred even when they were not British born. Tolkien had been brought from South Africa at the age of four; Lewis was a Belfast man schooled in England for whom, like his friend Tolkien, the Western Front had proved the deepest trauma of a largely bookish life; Charles Williams, an Oxford publisher who died in 1945, was a Londoner; Dorothy Sayers, who died a dozen years later, the daughter of an Anglican clergyman; and Owen Barfield a London solicitor who shared with his friends a passion for all things lexical, and above all for the etymology of words. This was emphatically, in its loyalties, a native school.

Its religion, though always Christian, was not precisely uniform. Charles Williams and Dorothy Sayers were touched by Anglo-Catholicism. Lewis was a mainstream Anglican who had angered Tolkien, on his conversion, by preferring Canterbury to Rome; but his title *Mere Christianity* (1952) summed up his disdain for all denominational differences, and he never accepted the charge of belonging to any one wing of the Church. John Heath-Stubbs, another Oxford man who may count as the poet of the group, was a lifelong Conservative and High Churchman in reaction to a boyhood spent attending a progressive school in the Isle of Wight. Events soon conspired to advance their cause. The peace of 1945 brought revelations of what a radical and atheistical regime like the Hitlerian could achieve in terms of human suffering, and it prompted a mood of religious revival throughout Western Europe, in Germany and beyond. *Titus Groan* (1946), the first of Mervyn Peake's three Titus books, is not exactly religious fiction, but its setting of Gothic nightmare is worlds away from any secular imagination, and its success is said to have surprised author and publisher alike. This was a mood that did not last; the secular spirit is natural, it is more than ever clear, to modern industrial states – so much so that it invades even the clergy. But the school of Tolkien was still notable in creating a large, sudden surface ripple in intellectual life: a surprising return to a sense of the supernatural and the transcendent that modern technology and modern philosophy, between them, were supposed to have finished off for good.

The group was a coterie, meeting for beer in an Oxford pub on Tuesday mornings and for readings in Lewis's college room on Thursday evenings; and it came close, for a time, to qualifying as a sect. Tolkien and Lewis had met as early as 1926; in 1939 Charles Williams had moved as a publisher from London to Oxford, and by the last years of the war Christian revival was in active literary life. Its inner lines of force are obscure. 'We had a common view,' Lewis once conceded in a letter, 'but we had it before we met,' insisting that no one ever influenced Tolkien: 'You might as well try to influence a bandersnatch.'[1] Dorothy Sayers may never have met Tolkien, though she knew Charles Williams and had been profoundly stirred, as a translator of Dante, by his *Figure of Beatrice* (1943). The theology of the group was sufficiently united by the fact that, amid a secular intelligentsia, it was after all a theology. And that was enough. Tolkien was a Catholic who never entirely ceased to resent Lewis's preference for Anglicanism; others were High Church; and Lewis, who always claimed to see religion as an escape from superstition rather than from atheism, held himself scrupulously above such disputes. His own model of churchly behaviour, he once remarked, was Russian Orthodox, where people sit, stand, kneel or lie flat, and 'no one takes the slightest notice of what anyone else is doing,'[2] the guiding motto in religion (as in life) being to mind your own business. Friends, he would have said, agree because they already agree, not because they persuade one another, and the achievement of the group was less to instruct in virtue or in doctrine than to reassure themselves, and others, that religion and modern literature can live together, and that there were those on earth – a precious few – of sympathetic piety and like mind.

That mind was anti-Modernist and (what is far different) anti-modern. Since its mood was anti-superstitious, and many twentieth-century superstitions – theosophy, yoga, Marx and Freud – are Modernistic, or count as such, that was perhaps only natural. Tolkien in his letters freely admitted, as a professor of English, to reading little of anything written since the Middle Ages, to taking no interest in the present state of English fiction, to disliking T. S. Eliot intensely, to finding Robert Graves an ass, and to thinking Browning's poems shallow and vulgar. Lewis was markedly less exclusive and less austere; but he had once borrowed a copy of Eliot's verse in 1926 from John Betjeman, then an unsatisfactory Oxford pupil, and it had enraged him – so much so that he had organised a cabal to write spoof verse in the Eliot manner to introduce into his quarterly *Criterion*. The joke came to nothing, as it deserved, but the hunger for a literary tradition more narrative and less diagrammatic, more reverent of ancient story and less of modern despair, survived to the end. To the starved world of pre-war Modernism the Christian revivalists promised sudden, limitless riches. Tolkien had finished *The Lord of the Rings* by 1949, though it was refused on his terms and did not begin to appear for another five years, on a non-royalty agreement – to be coolly received by reviewers at home and rapturously welcomed in that heartland of Anglo-Saxon romanticism, the United States of America. But it was an adolescent cult on both sides of the Atlantic before the 1950s were out: one of the great fictional bestsellers of the mid-century. Lewis began his Narnia stories for children in 1949, but he had been publishing fiction for adults since *Out of the Silent Planet* (1938), a mixture of space-fiction and theology that he was soon to extend into a trilogy, ending with *That Hideous Strength* (1945). His early lack of success as a poet ended in triumph as a novelist, polemicist and literary historian – careers he continued in triple tandem for the rest of his life, in Oxford and after 1954 in Cambridge. Where his friend Charles Williams had achieved only phantasmal fictions that struggled implausibly to marry realism and the supernatural, Lewis turned that improbable formula into stories that compel attention. By the mid 1950s, with Tolkien's prose epic and the Lewis trilogy in wide circulation, the fiction of Christian revival was a sudden, active contender in the world of letters. Technical experiments like stream-of-consciousness had died of inanition some years before, and they left few heirs; and the poetic tradition of Eliot had been abandoned even by Eliot, who by the 1950s was writing little but plays. A handful of reactionary dons, meanwhile, had improbably made their mark and attracted the ardour even of the young. Revival had won.

★   ★   ★

The revival was firmly based on story. Modernism had had no truck with narrative momentum; and Eliot's post-war plays, which began with *The Cocktail Party* (1950), were always more compelling as moral analysis than as plot. His own love of stories, though real enough, was private, almost furtive – he was a dedicated reader of the Sherlock Holmes stories, for example – but it would take a sharp eye, and a good memory, to notice the quotation from Conan Doyle's 'The Musgrave Ritual' buried in his pre-war play *Murder in the Cathedral*. Christian revival, by contrast, was openly partisan of narrative. Lewis, whose youthful enthusiasm had been for Norse sagas and the verse tales of William Morris, seems to have been converted to Christianity by considering whether the Christian myth might not, after all, be something more than a fiction. This was an understoried generation, and by the 1930s profoundly discontented with the literary starvation-diet of the age; virtuously repelled, too, by the sexual obsessions of literary

Freudians and D. H. Lawrence; and angry at the post-
ures and impostures of Modernism, as they saw it, and
the bloodless flimsiness of Bloomsbury fiction. A health-
cure, they held, may be healthy for a time, but it was
always hard to imagine any of them, at any time, with a
copy of Joyce's *Finnegans Wake* (1939) in hand. And then
the worm turned. One day, in desperation, Lewis said
to Tolkien: 'Tollers, there is too little of what we really
like in stories: I am afraid we shall have to write some
ourselves.'[3]

Story meant fable. The fiction of Tolkien and Lewis is
a compound of ancient fable – classical, Norse and
Wagnerian – with an eye cocked to modern reality, and
it might have been written to prove that there is a reality
beyond realism. *The Lord of the Rings* is a Wagnerian tale
partly domesticated – its style reminiscent, as befits an
Edwardian boy, of the Kipling who once wrote *Rewards
and Fairies* and delighted children with *Puck of Pook's
Hill*. Wagner in his day had preached purity of heart and
heroic deeds. Tolkien's epic is more like a romantic
reflection of pre-1914 British life and of those models of
manly virtue he had once witnessed and cherished, it
seems likely, in the grim camaraderie of the trenches in
the First World War. It is also playfully lexical, in a
manner that engagingly unites the bookish child and
the ageing professor of Anglo-Saxon, and its word-
games are totally unlike those of Joyce – more to do with
etymology than punning, more Germanic than Latin,
and ultimately populist and patriotic in their insistence
on how English arose out of its pre-Conquest roots. The
name Tolkien, he once remarked in a letter, is based on
the German word for foolhardy[4]: which is what, when
he finally had his huge romance published, he must
have supposed himself to be. But then it was a labour of
love. Nobody, he once remarked, believed him when he
said it was an attempt to create a world in which a

language agreeable to his own private aesthetic might be made to seem real, and even his childhood seems to have been enlivened by inventing as well as learning remote languages. But beyond all that, the book celebrates a concern that a later age was to call ecological. To the Victorian mind – and Tolkien, like Ivy Compton-Burnett, was born in 1892, and proudly a native of that age – a hatred of industrial capitalism was more naturally conservative, even Conservative, than radical – a wholly sensible view that might be worth recovering; and *The Lord of the Rings* is a conservative tract for green England and the moral attributes of a pre-industrial world. At the conclusion of *The Return of the King*, the third of the three books – Tolkien always denied they were a trilogy – Frodo and his friends ride back to their lost land, to discover that 'they cared about it more than any other place in the world', though its cottages and gardens have been laid waste and replaced by ugly new houses and factories belching smoke; and they defeat the ruffians who had defiled it and resume the kingdom of little men. That echoes a dream even nearer to his heart, perhaps, than Christian myth: a rural, unviolated England of cherished corners and familiar food and drink. *The Lord of the Rings* is a study in threatened cosiness, of loved haunts lost and daringly recovered. Begun in the 1930s, it must have seemed after 1940, during the Nazi occupation of continental Europe, as if nature were imitating the nightmare of art; and in the end it celebrates a victory.

Tolkien's romance was an amalgam, then, and a potent one; and its improbable success in his sixties lay not just in proving itself a bestseller but in making of itself the heart and mind of an international cult: a cult that was to spread to England from romantically-minded lands like California and the Antipodes. It filled a space long empty. Its little man-shaped creatures, first

paraded in *The Hobbit* (1937), hark back not just to
Kipling but far beyond him to medieval romance. Its
prose, often breezy and sometimes disturbingly vatic, is
a late reflection of Malory and Bunyan, and commonly
more vigorous than refined. Its passion for etymology,
real or invented, appealed to a vanishing social world
that adored word-games and crossword puzzles, and it
reflects Tolkien's early years as an editor of the *Oxford
English Dictionary*: in fact he thriftily reworked his philo-
logical papers into the texture of his fiction. His mock-
learned apparatus – appendices, maps of Middle-Earth
and indexes – suggest a sense of erudition amiably
mixed with bonhomie and fun; his no-nonsense Christianity a hunger for the spiritual and a yearning for roots.
The Lord of the Rings squanders small effort on stylistic
distinction or argumentative scruple. Its interlacing plot
reflects the medieval stories its author loved; its style,
bold and unsubtle, rails against the age of dictators and
the sour technocrats who governed Britain after the fall
of Hitler. It is one of those rare books the love of which
can easily turn into an addiction. Tempting, now that its
cult has faded, to conclude that it is a phenomenon in
the history of publishing rather than of fine writing. But
all that would be to ignore its symbolic potency in
defying a despotic age just lived through and narrowly
survived.

That defiance was at once conservative and Conservative. To turn Christian, in the 1930s and after, was to
declare for the past, and only Graham Greene among
notable pre-war literary converts to Rome was to maintain anything like a left-wing view of public affairs. The
only question here can be the shade of blue: but there
can be little doubt that, as befits Oxford men, the blue of
Christian revival tended to be dark. Lewis once remarked to a colleague during the Attlee premiership of
1945–51, and quite without irony, that it could not be

disputed that the prime minister was an agent of the Devil. He was notably more libertarian than Tolkien, for all that, who as a Catholic had supported Franco during the Spanish Civil War. Lewis was inclined to ground his grudging acceptance of democracy on the doctrine of original sin; Tolkien rejected it on the grounds that public virtue cannot be mechanised or formulated. But *The Lord of the Rings* is still a hidden diatribe against concentrated power, and it prefigures a fashion for ecology and small-is-beautiful. It is instructive to recall that the cause of conservation was conservative before it was ever radical. After all, it is about the conservation of the old and founded on a suspicion of the new.

Virtue, to such minds, was not institutional but inescapably personal. Like Swift they valued the generosity of the heart but not of law-makers, suspected all justice that was not severely retributive, and found confirmation for their faith in the fact that the bloody new tyrannies of Europe were more often atheistical than Christian. The Christian despotism of Louis XIV had been content with outward obedience rather than the subjection of the heart: Hitler and Stalin were mass-murderers because for them outward obedience was not enough. At that point the convictions of the Christian revivalists touch Orwell's and Koestler's, and overlap. But the secular mind looked to them a starved mind, desolate of passion because robbed of faith, and it never occurred to them to doubt that religion possesses and monopolises the spiritual life.

Christian revival was appropriately confessional, and there is no problem for the historian here of the secretive heart. This was a highly polemical school; its literary triumphs belong as much to the article or essay as to narrative; and its most private griefs and imaginings are by now part of the national and international consciousness. In the highly private world of mid-

century England, all this is astonishing. It is even, on
occasion, embarrassing, to anyone who retains a talent
to be embarrassed. Tolkien's romance is not a book for
the trained critic but for the enthusiastic semi-amateur
with an avidity for self-improvement; and in intention,
at least, it is essentially sexless. But Lewis's fiction *Till
We Have Faces* (1956) is the outcome of a private dream
that haunted him for decades, based on the ancient
myth of Cupid and Psyche, though it outpaces at times
his capacity to tell. So does *A Grief Observed* (1961),
seemingly a diary on the death of his wife, which breaks
every rule of decorum, classical or other. These were
minds so naturally paced to the business of authorship
that writing, from their middle years, must have
absorbed their waking hours, their conversations and
their dreams. They wrote as they breathed, and their
talk and their books were openly and unblushingly
self-revelatory.

Christian revival rose and fell, as a literary phase, in
the dozen years and more that followed the peace of
1945. Curious to think it overlapped with young realists
like Amis, Iris Murdoch and John Wain; still more
curious to think that Wain was a pupil of Lewis and a
junior member of Thursday evening meetings in his
Oxford college. (He was the young man who hoped
Tolkien would not read from the manuscript of *The Lord
of the Rings*). But the overlap in dates – Tolkien's book
began to appear in the same year as *Lucky Jim* – is
fortuitous, not significant, and the overlap in time was
not a collision of rival forces, rather the side-by-side
running of parallel tracks. The new realism owed nothing in technique or substance to the romances of
Tolkien and Lewis. It was not a derivative but another
way. 'I admired Lewis and his friends immensely,' Wain
reported years later in an autobiography; but 'already it
was clear that I did not share their basic attitudes,'[5]

which were Christian, conservative and anti-modern.
Romance and realism, if not exactly enemies, were
always opposites. The new realists took an unblinking
look at the human effects of welfare economics and the
emergent morality of a nation slowly quitting austerity
for affluence; the old romantics looked rather to recover
a world of fine fabling like Spenser's *Faerie Queene* or the
Victorian children's stories of George MacDonald.
Lewis read the great realists of the past, even of the
present, and he sometimes admired them; but he saw
their world as little better than a health-farm, held
himself bound by no especial duty to study his own
times, and longed for richer fare. 'What is the point of
keeping in touch with the contemporary scene?'[6] Since
God had created the universe, the artist should honour
Him by creating in his turn. He was ultimately forced to
see that the realistic tradition had proved too strong for
his friends and for him: 'Jack didn't kill the giant.' It was
great fun, all the same, to have tried.

★   ★   ★

At a larger distance, none the less, a pattern of partial
unity of purpose grows faintly visible, and the old
romancers and young realists of post-war Britain by
now look one in what they denied and defied, even if
they remain opposed in style and in the positives of
dogmatic faith.

Both, to begin, were hostile to the growing prospect of
a corporate state where power belongs less to parliament or cabinet than to organised interests such as
unions, multinationals, federations of employers, state
monopolies and established institutions like professional bodies. The Labour government that died in 1951 had
been tolerant of the corporate state, reverent of union
power and credulous of collectivism, and its spirit

persisted: by the 1970s half and more of those in full-time employment in Britain were employed, directly or indirectly, by the state. Authors, who are commonly self-employed, were naturally less forgiving of the corporate idea. Amis's Lucky Jim is not Tolkien's Frodo. He would not, one might guess, have destroyed the ugly new houses left by the occupying power of his homeland but lived in one of them; and though (like the heroes of Tolkien and Lewis) he likes beer as well as wine, he is not interested, as they were, in the cosy provincial life of the academic coterie. He wants London. His choice is wealth: he is at once the traditional hero of British fiction in search of a happy marriage and prosperity – Tom Jones or David Copperfield – and, in his brisk competitive zeal, the first fictional yuppie. He is Frodo not in what he wants but in what he casts aside: arbitrary power, reverence to the collective principle, deference to what is foreign and all hints of artistic pretension. But he is nothing of a nostalgic. He likes it here and he wants it now.

The romancers and the realists, again, were at one in their anti-Modernism. Charles Williams had been a friend of T. S. Eliot, but Lewis's distrust of Eliot had been implacable, and their first meeting in 1945, at Williams's instigation, had been no better than guarded, though they later joined as Anglicans in retranslating the Book of Common Prayer version of the Psalter. That Eliot was at once right-wing and Christian had counted for nothing, apparently, in earlier days. Lewis, in any case, was conservative rather than right-wing, and the alien world of Eliot's French-style royalism and his longstanding admiration for the Action Française never remotely appealed to him. Democracy might not be much, in his view, but everything else is worse; and a robber-baron, as he once remarked to the Marxist scientist J. B. S. Haldane, is better than an inquisitor, since greed sleeps easier than dogmatic certainty: 'where Mammon vacates the throne, how if Moloch takes his place?'[7] Eliot, in any case, looked to him the leader of a hated literary avant-garde; the world of his poetry contemptibly dry and thin, as Lewis imagined, his mind seemingly unstoried, his passion for Sherlock Holmes a secret too well kept to save him. And he never wrote a novel. Tolkien shared those views. He and Amis make an improbable duo, their births separated by thirty years and their convictions by still more. But at least they were united in wanting story and more story, and their worldly success suggested that by the 1950s the world was on their side. Modernism was played out, and it seemed absurd on all sorts of grounds that there should be no contemporary equivalent to *The Faerie Queene* or Trollope's Barchester novels. A nation had rediscovered its tradition of fiction – or rather, two traditions, the romantic and the realistic. It had come to its senses.

Its fiction, in a powerful sense, was patriotic. Tolkien's book celebrates the virtues of the common Englishman under heroic strain. Amis's third novel is called *I Like It Here* (1958), and when its hero stands reverently by the grave of Henry Fielding in Lisbon he acknowledges a debt at once literary and moral. The new fiction was contemptuous of modernistic tricks like stream-of-consciousness, which by the 1950s looked etiolated and, what is perhaps worse, un-English. Proust and Joyce were not Englishmen: Malory and Fielding were. In Tolkien and Amis alike – Christian and secular, conservative and radical – there sounds a common note of defiance and pride. Speaking of the Commonwealth at the time of Dunkirk in 1940, Churchill had talked of the old lion with her lion-cubs about her, and a lion that had beaten a unicorn must have ancient strengths that Modernism and Bloomsbury alike between the wars had failed to acknowledge or to note. To a generation emerging after victory, and to some of those who had taught them, those strengths and virtues seemed to have been underrated or ignored for too long.

4

The Coronation of Realism

In June 1953, with memorable pageantry, Elizabeth II was crowned queen, an event that promoted music rather than literature, among the arts, and design more than either. But though it served as a symbol, it symbolised something real; and it marks, aptly, a revival of realism in British fiction. Within a year of the event three first novels appeared in London that demanded an attentive scrutiny of the new age.

The three novels were *Lucky Jim*, *Under the Net* and *Lord of the Flies*. Their near-simultaneity was coincidence, in the sense of being beyond all collusion and foreknowledge, though all were by graduates of Oxford engaged in teaching and over the age of thirty. Two of them – Iris Murdoch and William Golding – are said to have composed a good deal of fiction before succeeding at last with a publisher; succeeding, as Golding once remarked, not because he had tried to please but because for once he stopped trying and wrote the book he had always wanted to write. Kingsley Amis's *Lucky Jim*, on the other hand, was only the second novel he had ever written, and he has since admitted that he was glad that the first was not published.

Along with other novelists, playwrights and poets, the three coronation novelists represent something plainly wider and looser than a coterie, though a Movement was promptly announced by a nameless journalist.[1] They had precursors. Philip Larkin had already published two novels – *Jill* (1946) and *A Girl in Winter* (1947) – before he established himself in 1955, with *The Less Deceived*, as the best poet of his generation; and John Osborne's first play ever to reach the public theatre, *Look Back in Anger* (1956), was written by an actor untouched by academia who had been writing for several years and a stranger to all of them. But though composed in ignorance of rival works, many of these writings were seen at the time, naturally and unhesitatingly, as the product of a single mood and of a single set of mind. Easy to say that the Movement was never more than a journalistic invention – the more so since its principals were (almost certainly) never together in one room. But it might be better to say that resemblances are all the more significant for that. A movement moves: it does not, and dares not, coalesce; and to capitalise it was no more than a modest journalistic hyperbole and a useful summary of an undoubted shift in literary taste.

Another collective title, the Angry Young Men, was to prove in the long term more accurate as prediction than description. *Lucky Jim* is too confident a book to be called angry, its predominating mood a scorn for a stuffy old order about to be swept away; but some of Amis's later novels, such as *Stanley and the Women* (1984), which was written by a sexagenarian, fizzle with fury. *Under the Net* and *Lord of the Flies* are too philosophical to be called angry, Golding (in any case) was always seen to be a spirit apart, and a few of these authors were strikingly young at their moment of first success. Their class origins, too, were rapidly fictionalised, but the notion of a sudden demotic invasion of polite letters can only be called extravagant. Literature – above all fiction – has never been a notably gentlemanly profession in Britain, as Dickens and H. G. Wells illustrate; and the Bloomsbury group had been upper middle-class rather than aristocratic. That did not prevent Somerset Maugham, in the sanctuary of a villa in the south of France, from shuddering at the private fantasy of a shaggy-haired mob seizing sudden sway in literary London – an effect, as he imagined, of the welfare state; and he was certain that their social origins were unprecedentedly humble. 'They have no manners,' he wrote spiritedly in a newspaper. 'They are scum'[2]: the sort of people, in fact, who become cabinet ministers. Strong words, to be believed and echoed through the 1950s and after by many critics at home and abroad, not least in the United States.

It is sobering to report that there is nothing in it. The myth that Britain is in some exceptional sense class-ridden dies hard, especially in America, perhaps because many are reluctant to acknowledge class-divisions and class-accents nearer home. The new novelists, in any case, were nothing like under-privileged; and as for the welfare state, it had been founded by the Asquith government after 1908 and was new, by the 1950s, only by recent extension. The Butler Education Act, designed to open higher education still further to the poor and unconnected, was not post-war, having been approved by a coalition government in 1944; and the new novelists cannot have owed their years at Oxford to R. A. Butler, since they were all undergraduates there before that year. No British university, in any case, is or ever has been socially exclusive, and the myth of an undergraduate Brideshead of champagne lunches set among gothic quadrangles is little more than an effect of Evelyn Waugh's selective social recollection. The poor have been students in Oxford and Cambridge continuously since the Middle Ages, and some of their ancient colleges were founded with statutes that explicitly excluded the rich.

There is nothing remotely unusual, in any case, about a British social upstart writing a novel. Dickens's social

origins were lowlier than those of anyone in the Movement, by a mile: not one of them ever worked in a
factory as a child, as he did, or even as an adult. Iris
Murdoch's father was a civil servant, Amis's an export
clerk, Larkin's a provincial city treasurer, and John
Wain's a dentist and an alderman. That is nothing like
the invasion of a new social class into British letters in
general or into fiction in particular. Talk about the new
working-class hero, too, looks odd when you consider
how few of its heroes were that; odder still if you think
back to the waifs and strays of Dickens, Smollett and
Defoe.

But the new novel was, in its own fashion, new. It
represented a sharp recall to a down-to-earth reality, an
openness to radical ideas and a frank rejection of refined
fictional experimentation, whether Bloomsbury-style or
other. Above all, it demanded accuracy. All that had its
1930s precursors, such as the early fiction of George
Orwell and Graham Greene; and in an open letter to
Elizabeth Bowen, written several years before the Movement was ever heard of, Greene had remarked that the
novelist has a simple duty to tell the truth and to get it
right: 'By truth I mean accuracy – it is largely a matter of
style'. Characters must not go white in the face, that is to
say, or tremble like leaves – 'not because these phrases
are clichés, but because they are untrue.'[3] Greene was in
mid career when he wrote that. But though his mind
was, and remained, romantically anti-Establishment, at
once Catholic and mildly left-wing, his fiction never
seemed impelled by any serious desire to alter the social
system of a nation from which, after the war, he was
willingly an exile, and his arguments concern rather the
writer's alleged duty to refuse all favours from the state
– even 'the bourgeois state', as he calls it – and to live in
romantic independence, royalties apart: surviving (in
Joyce's famous phrase) by silence and cunning. If the

soldier's duty is loyalty, Greene claimed, then the writer's is disloyalty.[4] That sounds more like a pose defiantly struck than a programme of reform: more Byron than Dickens. The new novelists, of the 1950s, by contrast, were authentic radicals in a Dickensian tradition; and in the post-war age realism, quite rightly, was felt to be radical.

The point, once obvious, has ceased to be that, and it may need to be restated. Realism is radical because any purposive attempt to change the world depends on a conviction that it can be described, even that it has been described; and it is the chosen task of realism to describe. To frame a programme, a manifesto, or a legislative act, a dim sense of injustice is not enough, still less an attitude of defiance. That is why self-conscious fictional experimentation like stream-of-consciousness tends in its social effects to be conservative, whatever its aspirations; and the later fiction of Joyce and Virginia Woolf cannot be seen to embody any serious proposal to change the world, or to represent a belief that the world could ever be changed. Such fiction marches happily with political impassivity and an acquiescence in things as they are. Realism, to be sure, is not restricted to one's own world, as Defoe proved when he wrote *Crusoe*. William Golding's second novel, *The Inheritors* (1955), and his favourite, is about the historically remote world of Neanderthal man, conversing in cries and grunts and on the point of being supplanted by smooth and hairless superior beings; his third, *Pincher Martin* (1956) drowns its hero on the second page and recounts his thoughts in the rest. There are no easy party affiliations here. But Golding's fictional imagination is plainly disturbing to established assumptions, to complacency, to amiable acceptance. It is untrifling and serious, even open to the charge of blasphemy. As Salman Rushdie perceptively remarked

several years before *Satanic Verses* (1988) forced him into
hiding to escape Muslim extremists outraged by his
handling of the Prophet, realism can break your heart.

It would be misleading to present the revival of
realism as a total abandonment of technical experiment.
All new starts are in some sense experimental, a revived
realism not least; and it is after all mildly experimental,
in a way, to return to a half-deserted tradition forged in
England two hundred years before in the age of the
Hanoverians. Realism had flourished with Defoe,
Richardson, Fielding and Smollett, and these were to be
the presiding deities of the new British novel. Angus
Wilson claimed to have read and reread Richardson's
Clarissa, for all its immense bulk, starting at the age of
eighteen, admiring above all its triumphant creation of
fantasy out of realistic detail – a realism made transcendent – though he also admired the 'God's eye view' of
the great nineteenth-century novels.[5] Fielding, Amis
once remarked, showed that fiction can uphold a moral
seriousness 'without evangelical puffing and blowing';
his *Take a Girl Like You* (1960) has been aptly called a
modernised replay of Richardson's *Pamela*[6]; and when
asked by a journalist which of the great novelists of the
past he felt the closest affinity with, he replied reverently: 'With Fielding, though it seems a gross
impertinence. . .'.[7] John Wain, who is said to reread
Johnson's *Rasselas* every year, has the heroine of his first
novel, *Hurry on Down* (1953), call herself Moll Flanders
because she has just been reading Defoe's novel and
scents a resemblance to herself; and Iris Murdoch, who
seldom reads twentieth-century fiction at all, is profoundly immersed in the great realistic fiction of earlier
ages, whether English, French or Russian. *Under the Net*
(1954), her first published fiction, is technically speaking
a memoir-novel like *Crusoe* or *Moll Flanders*, being composed as autobiography in the first person; and *The Sea,*

the Sea (1978), like *Crusoe*, is in part a diary where the narrator – male, as usual – is himself so unaware as he writes of the astonishing end there will be to kidnapping his lost love that the reader is as surprised as he when it finally unfolds: an audacious exploitation of the fictional memoir never attempted by Defoe himself. Golding's *Lord of the Flies* (1954) is in the third person, though like Defoe's most famous novel it is about an island marooning; but *Rites of Passage* (1980) – the first of the Tarpaulin trilogy – is a memoir-novel, composed not just in the first person but in a pastiche of the English of the Napoleonic wars, especially in its sea-terms – a sort of 'sub-Jane Austen language', as he has breezily put it. In post-war Britain, it is clear, fiction consciously returned in technique, in morality, even occasionally in style, to its Hanoverian roots.

There are two eighteenth centuries vivid to the modern literary consciousness. The one, familiar between the wars to Bloomsbury and the Sitwells, was mannered, urbane and aphoristic, dressed in silks and powdered wigs and usually more French than English. That imaginary age, and not the robust world of the new novelists of the 1950s, was what Evelyn Waugh celebrated in the opening paragraph of *The Ordeal of Gilbert Pinfold* (1957) when he predicted that the present age of English novelists would one day be 'valued as we now value the artists and craftsmen of the late eighteenth century': a late-rococo world where Victorian exuberance had been replaced by 'elegance and variety of contrivance'. Himself apart, Waugh may have had Anthony Powell and L. P. Hartley in mind, those careful craftsmen of post-war fiction. The first sentence of Hartley's *The Go-Between* (1953), which appeared when its author was nearly sixty, has by now entered into the valhalla of literary allusion:

The past is a foreign country: they do things different-
ly there,

where the vocabulary, the syntax, even the punctuation
suggest a high honing of stylistic effect reminiscent of
Gibbon rather than Swift, of Beckford rather than Defoe.

That is one eighteenth century. The other is the far
gamier world of Defoe and Fielding, and it is that
memory that Amis and Murdoch revived. Such fiction,
unconcise and more naturally given to carnality than
wit, had been unashamedly dominated by story, and it
was characteristically fast-paced and impatient of extended description, whether of scene, of motive or of
mind. Dismissive of anything that is not narrative, it
would have seen E. M. Forster's gentle and reluctant
admission – 'Yes – oh dear yes – the novel tells a story' –
as merely faddy. Narrative is suddenly, and once again,
the blood and guts of fiction, and Waugh's remark that
'the exuberant men are extinct' was out of date even as
he wrote, though only just.

A sudden contempt for technical finesse was perhaps
only natural. The ordinary stuff of realism at its most
immediate seldom needs elaboration, since it is something the novelist shares with his reader. There is small
need to explain; and the whole activity, so the novelist
may reasonably feel, is self-justifying. 'A blow on behalf
of the ordinary universe' Golding once called his own
fiction in a BBC interview, explaining what he had
thought himself to be about when he wrote *Pincher
Martin*. The new novel was rootedly ordinary, and the
refined reflections of a Mrs Dalloway walking down
Bond Street, for example, or the fantastic world of
Tolkien's Frodo, are equally alien to it. As Golding was
to remark in Stockholm in 1983, on receiving the Nobel
prize for literature, fiction has far more to do with the
general mind of mankind than with the writer's own

quirks and obsessions: 'not just what the writer is thinking, but what a huge segment of the world is thinking.' Words, he went on,

> may allow man to speak to man, the man in the street to speak to his fellow, until a ripple becomes a tide running through every nation – of common sense, of simple healthy caution – a tide that rulers and negotiators cannot ignore . . .

teaching us to be temperate in ourselves and moving mankind as a whole 'a little nearer the perilous safety of a warless and provident world.'[8] Such fiction concerns the attainable, un-utopian virtue of daily life.

Golding's own fictional worlds, unlike Amis's or Murdoch's, have tended to be enclosed, which may be natural to one whose early experience has been in naval life and schoolteaching; and unlike theirs, powerfully concerned with the perils of code-breaking and a sense of shame. Iris Murdoch's fiction has centred rather on a search for goodness, most often by means of loving relationships; Amis's with a sense of decorum and indecorum – with social habits and rules made, altered and broken by the changing generations. All that, though it eschews propaganda, still sounds programmatic, and the new novel of the 1950s was plainly a committed literature. It defined itself sharply against a dilapidated Modernism that had denied knowledge and flirted with radical scepticism. In his Harvard thesis of 1916 T. S. Eliot had claimed any knowledge of reality to be little more than a perilous mental construct: 'we are forced to admit that the construction is not always completely successful,' being 'always about to fall apart.'[9] But it is an odd kind of belief that one accords to propositions one cannot claim to know; and Eliot's talk of mental constructs, plainly an uncomfortable compromise in itself, sits oddly with his intense dogmatism about morality and public affairs. The radical instability of the Modernist view of knowledge, whether moral or social, was manifest; and if Iris Murdoch, among the new novelists, was alone in her capacity as a professional philosopher to counter poor arguments with better, it was equally clear that no one had to be a philosopher to see that the scepticisms of the inter-war years were implausible and ultimately self-contradicting.

That is the more rational side of the debate. Some other aspects of the anti-Modernism of the new fiction, it must be conceded, were at times more chauvinistic than reasoned. Modernism always had an irremediably alien air about it, having reached England at around the turn of the century in the hands of immigrants: Conrad from Poland, Eliot and Pound from the United States, Wyndham Lewis from somewhere vaguely transatlantic. It had rejoiced, as alien coteries naturally do, in its own intellectual isolation; and in disdaining narrative, or at least fast-paced narrative, it had disavowed one of the native strengths of the tradition. James Joyce, its greatest master of fiction, never settled in England, though he chose to live and die a British subject. Some alien imports are quickly acclimatised into artistic traditions that last for decades or centuries, and nobody bothers if most of Shakespeare's sources were continental, if porcelain came to England from China by way of Saxony, or if almost all the literary kinds the English tradition has excelled in, excepting only the detective story, have been borrowed from abroad. But Modernism had the odd distinction of starting foreign and staying foreign. Regarded as a whole, it was unassimilable. It is even a question whether it ever seriously sought assimilation.

That is not to say that it left no trace, with its demise, and the anti-Modernism of the new novelist was not instinctive or immediate but of slow and uncertain growth. Some of the new realists began their literary lives in homage to Eliot, Joyce or Samuel Beckett. Iris Murdoch when young wrote Beckett a fan-letter, and her first published book was a critical study of Sartre (1953). In the 1950s John Wain proposed that the task of the Movement in verse was to consolidate the tradition of Eliot and Pound. Philip Larkin began as a poet in the tradition of W. B. Yeats, and only slowly came to see that Thomas Hardy, not Yeats, was to be his poetic master. After flirting with Modernism in his earlier fiction, John Fowles was to deride the whole idea as late as 1982, with *Mantissa*, which makes elaborate fun of the tradition of Joyce and argues that fiction may find it hard even to survive the grinding tedium of the *nouveau roman*. 'At least the French are doing their best to kill the whole stupid thing off for good,' the heroine remarks; and when her lover solemnly tells her that modern fiction can only be about the difficulty of writing fiction, she asks why writers bother to put their names on title-pages. Two years later Julian Barnes, in *Flaubert's Parrot* (1984), entertained the same subversive point in a novel of impish erudition: the past, he suggests in his opening chapter, is rather like a greasy piglet, and anyone who tries to seize it is bound to look ridiculous. The extremists of Modernist scepticism, as in *la nouvelle critique*, might proclaim the Death of the Author and deny that intention was ever knowable: but authors were still interrogated, and after some fashion known. The trouble is that the past, like the present, is in the end not optional, and it is natural to be curious about it. One has to understand it to live at all. No wonder, then, if realism, which makes a claim to know past and present in unequivocal terms, returned to fiction and repossessed the field. It was like melody in music. Once tried, it was too potent ever to be abandoned for good.

The flirting remains, perhaps to assure the sophisticated reader that Modernism has been absorbed and
transcended, not merely ignored or forgotten. Fowles's
finest novel, *The French Lieutenant's Woman* (1969), is
decorated with parodistic devices far less integral than
in Joyce's *Ulysses*, as if a technique needed to be aped
and mocked in order to be exorcised. When Paul Sayer
won a literary prize for a grimly realistic first novel, *The
Comforts of Madness* (1988), in which an insane narrator
never speaks, he confessed that it was an imitation of
Beckett's *Malone Dies* (1956): 'I could see how he avoided
telling about the main thing: that's something I tried to
do in my book,'[10] though it does not read like Beckett.
Modernism may be a spectre at the feast of the new
realism, and little more. But it can make its presence felt,
at least to those with imaginations to see: first admired,
then feared, and finally mocked and looted for fragmentary hints and occasional ideas.

That rejection, in the first instance, was anti-
cosmopolitan. A youthful flirtation with Marx and Sartre
might be allowed, even encouraged, as wild oats are
sown before they are gathered, and both Amis and Iris
Murdoch were teenage communists; but the new realism, simply because it was realist, was bound to take its
lessons from nearer home. Its ordinary universe, as
Golding called it, was highly unlike Yeats's candle-lit
salon or Pound's cloak and broad-brimmed hat. It
cooked and washed the dishes afterwards and preferred
pubs to cafés, and its fiction cheerfully describes a world
of kitchen squalor and bedsit intimacies. Reviewing
Pincher Martin, Amis once mildly reproached Golding
for failing to 'turn his gifts of originality, of intransigence, and above all of passion to the world where we
have to live',[11] since the novel is set remotely on an
island in the Atlantic. The reproof, justified or not, is
significant. The new novel usually starts from where

one is, seldom from a vision of a lost world or future utopia. Beryl Bainbridge has told how she finds plots for her novels by visiting the newspaper repository of the British Library in north London, looking out old daily papers for crimes and bizarre happenings. Reality is what is going on under your nose. 'You find something,' she once remarked in an interview, 'and then you wrap your own life around it.'

Amis's reproof to Golding was in the end too absolute. Realism is at most an ingredient of fiction, in any case, and never more — even when it is the principal ingredient — and to call a novel realistic can mean no more than that one element has tended to prevail. It is like flour in cooking: no recipe consists of flour alone, though many utterly depend on it to be what they are. To imagine that the revived realism of the 1950s and after excluded other possibilities, then, is to misunderstand its nature, and the chauvinism of the school was always something of a pose. Realism welcomes admixture; it even requires it. It forbids its own purity. All fictions, as Henry James remarked in a preface, even the most realistic, need to be artificially opened and closed — 'relations stop nowhere' — so that artifice is its essence, first and last. Realism is not a narrowing technique, then, but a liberating, and there is no fictional technique it does not, on occasion, readily combine with. It embraces multitudes. Iris Murdoch has spoken of novels as tending to be either crystalline or journalistic; and the journalistic, which she practises, sounds like a free-wheeling and ever-hospitable realism: 'a large, shapeless, quasi-documentary object ... telling with pale conventional characters some straightforward story enlivened with empirical facts.'[12] Omit the pallor, which is an odd and perhaps over-modest intrusion into the account, and that sounds like Defoe or Dickens or Proust — or Murdoch: its converse, the crystalline novel, being 'a small quasi-allegorical object portraying the human condition,' which sounds like *Rasselas*, Waugh's *Decline and Fall* or Orwell's *Animal Farm* – not to mention the fiction of Muriel Spark, which can be artfully, even heartlessly, diagrammatic. A year or two later, expanding on her analysis, Iris Murdoch dubbed the journalistic novel 'loose and cheerful', adding gaily that she was inclined to start writing a novel in the hope that 'a lot of people who are not me are going to come into existence in some wonderful way'[13] – though frustrated, sometimes, by the prevailing theoretical power of her own philosophical mind. But then realism, as she knows, like journalism, does not exclude analysis: in fact her first book, *Sartre*, had ended in a mild sense of exasperation against philosophy itself, which she believed had frustrated Sartre by making him unable to write a great novel, 'a tragic symptom of a situation which afflicts us all'. We know the human individual to be unique, that is, and uniquely precious, but the net of abstraction can forbid the fiction-writer to present it as either precious or unique.

Months later, in her first published novel, she finally broke with the dominance of abstraction; and *Under the Net* dances lyrically and playfully around the philosophical idea suggested in its title. Abstraction and theory imprison us, or try to do so, as if in a net, and the novel tests and demolishes the allegedly superior power of abstract thought over a thinking and feeling life: 'how far conceptualizing and theorizing divide you from the thing that is the object of theoretical attention.'[14] That sounds rather like Wittgenstein's famous injunction in *Philosophical Investigations* (1953) – 'Don't think, look' – and it is marvellously coincidental that Wittgenstein's greatest book, too, appeared posthumously – he died in 1951 – in coronation year. 'No theory explains everything,' she remarks elsewhere, 'yet it is just the desire to explain everything which is the spur of theory.'[15] With her first fiction, then, Iris Murdoch joined the ranks of theorists who are part sceptical of theory; and though her writings never lose the marks of a philosophical training, they suggest a training that has been lived and effectively outlived, a sense of theory turned questioning and whimsical. 'There are some parts of London which are necessary and others which are contingent' is quite a good joke, though perhaps you would have to be a philosopher as well as a Londoner to see the point of it.

To understand the world, then, and understand it well enough to contrive to live in it, there is no one way: not fact, not theory, not particularity, not abstraction; and explanations of whatever kind are not universal answers, merely part of a progressive and accumulative act of learning and knowing. The mythical, for example, as she argues, is not 'something extra', since men live in myth and symbol all the time, and one myth can be needed to free the mind from another – liberating it to contemplate goodness, which has no ultimate purpose beyond itself. The only authentic way to be good is to be good 'for nothing': that was to become the ringing insistence of her finest treatise, *The Sovereignty of Good* (1970). In this author philosophy and fiction continuously interact and are, at most, only formally distinct. Her philosophy can at moments read like a novel, in its invented illustrations; her novels, in their discursive passages, much like philosophy in unbuttoned mood. But then the severely discursive is ultimately inadequate, as she knows, which is why mankind needs ever more fictions to live by, why there have to be new novels as well as old. If a truth is complicated, a character remarks in *An Accidental Man* (1971), 'you have to be an artist not to utter it as a lie'. That, though it is from a novel, sounds like one for the seminar. But the seminar could never do the whole of what a novel does, since theory falsifies where stories teach wisdom. Fiction arises here out of a lively discontent with systems and systematisers. Philosophy is very small, as she once told a fellow-philosopher and, what is worse, 'counternatural'.[16] Fiction, then, is rather like architecture or plumbing – a necessary art.

★   ★   ★

A duty to describe is the moral hallmark of the new novel. In an age when avoiding the point had grown to be associated with Modernism and was ceasing to look like an amusing trick, realism looked courageous, unblinking and unbowdlerising. W. H. Auden had remarked years before, in a sonnet called 'The Novelist' (1939), how alarmingly inclusive the fiction-writer looks, compared with the poet:

> . . . he must
> Become the whole of boredom, subject to
> Vulgar complaints like love, among the Just
>
> Be just, among the Filthy filthy too . . .

That was written twenty years and more before the trial and acquittal of D. H. Lawrence's *Lady Chatterley's Lover* in October–November 1960 – an event that made more headlines than practical difference, though it marks a convenient turning-point in British official attitudes to literary obscenity. The new novel is just and filthy. It is not for the squeamish, but equally it is not for the merely despairing. It entertains the possibility of amelioration and even of cure. To be modernist, a post-war French aphorist once remarked, is to mess about with what cannot be mended (*'bricoler dans l'incurable'*). That is not an assumption made by Amis or Golding or

Murdoch, and that is the plain sense in which they are not Modernists. They believe the world can be made better, and that literature can help to make it so. They are not for messing about.

In texture the new novel is comic. The journalist who in 1954 invented the term 'The Movement' aptly called the temper of its fiction 'sceptical, robust and ironic'. That, too, was a return to roots, if one accepts that comedy (and above all social comedy) is the true genius of the nation and the thing it does best. The point is not new: Samuel Johnson believed that Shakespeare's comedies reveal a profounder instinct than his tragedies: 'his tragedy seems to be skill, his comedy to be instinct'. Comedy, in any case, is not necessarily optimistic, and it can tellingly present a tragic world – a point readily overlooked by those who confuse literary forms like tragedy with states of mind like a tragic view of life, as if over-obsequious to a terminology or eager to be confused by one. Some tragedy consoles, after all, and it is arguable that some of its consolations are facile and false. The matter of fiction, in any case, given that it aims at realism, does not readily divide according to the classic view. 'All sorts of tragic experiences,' Amis has remarked, 'have comic capsules secreted in them.'[17] Comedy is radical, too, in the sense of forcing the reader to reconsider traditional reverences: tragedy can flatter and soothe with an assurance that even in the dungeon or on the scaffold the heroic mind is invulnerable.

Comedy, what is more, is arguably a higher skill, as many a performer knows. 'A concert pianist is allowed a wrong note here and there,' Amis observed in his introduction to *The New Oxford Book of Light Verse* (1978), 'a juggler is not allowed to drop a plate.' The most refined skills, in that robust view, are not in the Royal Albert Hall but at the end of the pier. All that suggests a fierce and self-justifying pride in comic technique; and the technical resources of the new realism, though sometimes self-effacing, are not trivial. *Lucky Jim* may survive in the memory as a series of farcical moments, but it is also a tightly plotted novel; *The Green Man* (1969), a nightmarish ghost-story, has one of the most ingenious plots in English fiction. If the British are a whimsical nation, their whimsies can be well researched and well rehearsed, like the epigrams of an accomplished conversationalist, and as carefully planned. That, to be sure, is not the manner of Anthony Burgess, a Manchester-born novelist of Catholic upbringing who has lived much of his abundantly creative life in Italy and Monte Carlo; and his *A Clockwork Orange* (1962) and *Earthly Powers* (1980), though lit with humour, suggest a darker and more haunted vision. But then Burgess, though a master of many moods, seems to mistrust the comic, and believes that entertainment falsifies the world by concentrating on matter rather than manner. That, like his exile, suggests a soul apart. By and large, the new novel since 1953 has moved most naturally between social comedy and farce.

The sources of that mood – sceptical, robust, ironic – though ultimately eighteenth-century, are far more immediate than Fielding or Smollett. Open one of the new novels of the 1950s and read a page at random, and one is reminded of the inter-war comic fictions of P. G. Wodehouse or the early social novels of George Orwell. Lucky Jim as an over-night visitor drunkenly burning his host's sheets with his cigarette-ends, and desperately trying to disguise the damage with a pair of scissors, is farcical in a Wodehouse sort of way, though the social rank of the characters is down more than a notch or two. The scene is Orwellian, too, not just in its suburban setting but in its prevailing emphasis on a pained sense of demeaning social inferiority and skimping poverty. But there the resemblances end, and an Amis novel offers a far more carnal world than Wodehouse or even early Orwell, its sexuality gamier by a mile. Comic skills are exploited with an evident pride in technique, like the juggler tossing his plates, but there is a sudden expansion in range. The unmentionable is now to be mentioned: in fact, six years before *Lady Chatterley's Lover* went into paperback, it is wheeled centre-stage. Radical, flippant and brash, the 1950s novel takes avid pride in its accuracy; and in presenting the post-war world with a compelling image of itself, it cannot plausibly omit the predominating drive of sex.

Its hero is all of a kind with that world of austerity and shortages, and the fashionable search for the working-class hero may have led critics into missing some of the deeper connections here. There is nothing new about working-class heroes or heroines in English fiction; what is new in post-war Britain, on the contrary, is the slow fade-out of a class of odd-jobbers and wage-earners of modest habits and narrow horizons familiar to all earlier ages of British fiction. Post-war Britain is not the age when the working-class hero arrived on the literary stage but rather the moment when, with some evident reluctance, he left it. The new hero may start out in life as untenured or a drifter – seldom as a wage-earner – but he settles down. He was a yuppie decades before the word was invented, and his stated objects in life were self-promotion and a settled life. And that, after all, is a pattern entirely familiar in British fiction. It is Tom Jones, it is Edward Waverley, it is David Copperfield. In a last chapter the young rover turns, and by his own eager wish, to settle into a life of married affluence. These are fictions about experimenting with an impecunious and occasionally feckless life of adventure, and then giving it up. An escapade or two can help to teach what the world is like, and even why it is what it is; but novels in this age-old tradition of English fiction, though often radical, are in no way revolutionary. Things are what they are, and mankind is unchanging, even if men and women change as individuals from moment to moment. Scott's Captain Waverley, as a southern Whig, is momentarily infatuated with the Jacobite Highlands, but he returns south and is pardoned for his treason. The heroes of *Under the Net* and *Lucky Jim* follow a broadly similar path, bemused at first by false starts and coming by the end to see the social world as it is: various, unstereotypable, kaleidoscopic and as fast-shifting as the shades of an opal, but in the end a place to settle into and improve rather than a system to defy. The game is self-promotion, and a game is more fun if you observe the rules. It is then, and only then, after all, that you can hope to play it better and to win.

★   ★   ★

That learning process – a sort of out-of-school education in life itself – is above all a study in embarrassment; and the embarrassable hero is abundant in comedy and alive outside it, even in the final awesome scene of Golding's *Lord of the Flies*. That scene, as Golding has often told, was the first he conceived of, and he invented the rest of the book with the conclusion already in mind; and it tells of a frightened boy 'tensed for more terrors' who staggers to his feet to find not his tormentors but an officer in a white-topped cap:

> He saw white drill, epaulettes, a revolver, a row of gilt buttons down the front of a uniform. A naval officer stood on the sand,

and as the island burns he tells of two boys killed, and childish tears flow:

The officer, surrounded by these noises, was moved and a little embarrassed. He turned away to give them time to pull themselves together; and waited, allowing his eyes to rest on the trim cruiser in the distance.

And so the novel ends in total shock, much like occupied Europe in 1945, with a sense of all civility and order disrupted and about to be restored, and not at all like the cosy world of Coral Island. Embarrassment is usually comic, especially in fiction. But here Golding offers the extremest instance of how it might be tragic too.

The theme is so persistent as to invite analysis. Embarrassment, it seems clear, is a major concern of the British psyche, and the dreams the British dream, if opinion-polls are to be believed, tend to be about social embarrassment, with amorous fantasy playing only a disappointingly minor role; and if that is to be taken in evidence, then it may be said to represent a more powerful obsession than sex. The deepest psychic hurts are to a sense of decorum, and *Lord of the Flies* ends with a hint of normal life to come: the boys will be scrubbed and dressed, one may be sure, their barbarities and indecencies put behind them, and sent back to school. Civility has been shattered on Golding's island. But it will return.

Doing all that means doing the Right Thing, and any such notion, in life or in fiction, depends on a shared acceptance of what the Right Thing is. That acceptance is not a characteristic of British life, merely a truth of it. Any settled society has right and wrong ways of living together – not least revolutionary societies, which tend to be conformist beyond all others. The oddity of the British achievement has been to turn its sense of social conformity into an international commodity. Its heroes do not characteristically commit suicide or ride off into the sunset: they settle down, marry, and make comfortable and elaborate treaties with the world they live in. *Lucky Jim* ends with Jim getting a wife and a City job. Idle to say that such conformity is merely British: if it were so, the world would not so readily understand British fiction or buy it; and buy it does, whether as novels, films or TV serials. Waugh's *Brideshead Revisited* in the 1970s was watched across the face of the globe on television screens, like Galsworthy's *Forsyte Saga* before it. British realism is distinctive not in being realistic but in being exportable, embarrassment and all; and it is hard to resist the conclusion that the world buys it, including the American and Soviet worlds, because it is curious about what it is to be British. The shoreline that appears from the deck of the Calais packet is a fabled shore; and if a language is a dialect with an army, as somebody once said, then English is a dialect famed not just for its armaments but for its gentility and civic virtue.

Such international curiosity is far from new. Defoe and Richardson enjoyed it in the eighteenth century, Dickens in the next. It seems worth asking why, though it remains a question hard to answer, and impossible to answer in strictly literary terms. Social embarrassment, duly fictionalised, is an odd commodity to export, and it does not figure in official balance-of-payments figures; but it has been selling around the world since Fielding's *Tom Jones* and Scott's *Waverley*, not to mention Wodehouse's Bertie Wooster. Wooster, after all, in the inter-war Jeeves stories, was eternally trying to do the Right Thing and succeeding (if at all) only on the last page of the story. That too is what Charles Ryder does in Waugh's *Brideshead*, more or less, or Guy Crouchback in *Sword of Honour*; or Amis's Lucky Jim; or the savagely dishonoured hero of Golding's Tarpaulin trilogy. Embarrassment is under no obligation to be comic, though it is most naturally that, and as a fictional theme it is of inexhaustible power and seemingly unending appeal.

★   ★   ★

The political aspects of the new fiction are hardly easier
to generalise. William Golding, the oldest of the new
novelists, has told how his first novel emerged from
reflecting, as so many in the 1940s reflected, how readily
Hitler and his National Socialists had revived barbarism
in our times, and in a modern and advanced industrial
state. The thought was (and is) unnerving, and it
illustrates how close realism sits to radical analysis, how
misplaced the critical stricture that it is merely cosy. *Lord
of the Flies* is a novel about English schoolboys marooned
on a desert island – a Defoe-like subject, though unlike
Crusoe it uses the third person – but reversing Defoe, it
tells of their rapid descent into savagery, totem-worship
and the childish joys of torture and terror. There is a
Nazi in everyone, so schoolmaster Golding suggests,
and there since childhood; and civilisation is no more
than the thinnest of thin veneers, as Hitler showed,
masking a base, innate craving to rule and be ruled. The
point is unrelenting and sharp. And yet Golding is
nothing like a political novelist in terms of British
domestic politics, and his views about political parties,
whatever they are, are not publicly a part of his fiction.

With Amis and Iris Murdoch the matter is more lucid;
and both can be seen, by now, as socialist novelists who
at varying pace soon ceased to be that. John Wain –
another Movement novelist – is said to have voted
Conservative as early as 1951, before he ever published
a book,[18] as if silently laying down a marker for the
future: but then that was in the days of Winston
Churchill. Iris Murdoch's war-time communism had
given place, well before her first novel ever appeared, to
an interest in Sartre's Existentialism: a natural stepping-

stone, in the 1940s, along a well-trodden path that leads
out of the simplifying preconceptions of Marxism; and
though earlier partisan interests flickered back half into
life in the 1960s, during the Vietnam war, she had
already abandoned Marx, and publicly, before the 1950s
were out. 'The salt itself,' she remarked sadly of socialism as early as 1958, 'seems to have lost its savour.'[19]
Reality, in any case, is not 'a given whole', as she wrote
soon after her disillusionment; that is why one is
'forever at odds with Marxism'.[20] A dogma that once
looked profound had been shown to be no more than a
simplistic diagram; and social reality is too complex, in
the end, to be embraced by any single theory of history
or of class. There *is* no class-war in advanced industrial
states, in any case; and the village idiot posted at the
town gate to welcome the Messiah, though never out of
work, is always likely to get bored with the job. That
rejection of simplicity came soon. 'It doesn't apply,'
Kingsley Amis remarked to himself as an adolescent
Marxist on joining the army during the war and glanc-
ing around the barracks at his new comrades. Life is far
more richly graded and shaded, in reality, than terms
like working-class and middle-class allow.

The shift of Amis's mind, thoughtful and unphilo-
sophical as it is, has been broadly a pattern to others of
his age. An ex-Marxian socialist in post-war Oxford, he
was to avow as late as 1957, in an address to the Fabian
Society called *Socialism and the Intellectuals*, that he had
voted Labour in every election since 1945, and 'unless
something very unexpected happens, I shall vote
Labour to the end of my days – however depraved the
Labour candidate may be, and however virtuous his
opponent.' That Something Very Unexpected, whatever
it was, happened shortly afterwards: by the 1960s Amis
was a figure of the New Right, and by the late 1970s
publicly Thatcherite. But that, after all, is to tread a path

that many trod. In 1979, similarly, Iris Murdoch remarked she was glad Labour lost; and she was voting Conservative, not without reservations, by the 1980s.

It might be rash to conclude that all that represents a rejection of radicalism; better, perhaps, to say that it is the sense of radicalism itself that changed. By the 1970s it was no longer obvious that socialism was radical. With over half the British labour force by then state-employed, whether directly or indirectly, competitive private enterprise in a dynamic style inspired by Japan, West Germany and the United States had come to look to many, and with some reason, like a radical option. Competition, as more and more noticed, can favour the poor in a way state monopolies are never likely to do; in fact it is precisely through concentrated economic power, not least in the great nationalised industries and services, that the rich can sometimes best thrive. Socialism-for-the-rich had by the 1970s ceased to be a mere phrase and become a visible fact. Welfare provision, too, can be higher in the capitalist West than in the socialist East, as the two Germanies illustrate; and the migration of the poor across the Iron Curtain, as many remarked, has not been in the direction of socialism. By the 1970s the goal-posts of political debate had been momentously shifted. A century earlier Sidney Webb, in *Fabian Essays* (1889), had argued that socialism was both efficient and irreversible. That was a view common enough by the 1940s, even among anti-socialists. But it was widely abandoned by the 1970s, a decade that historians may come to dub the graveyard of the socialist idea. In those years socialism finally ceased to look undeniably left-wing, whether east or west of the Iron Curtain; and if fiction changed its politics in that age, so did the world around it. It is the natural business of realism, after all, to reflect the world; and if realism did not cease to be radical, radicalism turned realistic. Competition, it is now clear, unlike monopoly, can be highly radical in the sense of destructive of traditional interests. As early as 1958 Iris Murdoch had perceptively observed that 'there is nothing in between' the technicalities of socialism and its highly simplistic morality:[21] argumentatively speaking, that is, you cannot get from central planning to such ideals as equality of opportunity or of condition. That was a truth the British learned by living it. And if the discovery radicalised its parties, not least the Conservatives, and left Britain without a genuinely conservative party in parliament or in the country, that odd effect of the demise of socialism passed almost unnoticed in an age eager to recover and proclaim the competitive principle.

* * *

Fiction itself traces the shift from the collective to the individual, from respect for the state to respect for the person.

The new English novel is above all about the search for goodness. With Golding, exceptionally, that can mean a long backward glance into history or even prehistory – to the world of lost innocence of Neanderthal man in *The Inheritors*, or to the pre-industrial world of the sailing ship in the Tarpaulin trilogy. In others it more commonly invites a searching look into the here-and-now, or at least into worlds close enough to be remembered. Golding and Murdoch represent the opposite poles of fictional genius: the one imposing a commanding pattern on his narratives, as if in allegory, the other (at her best) exploring a moral hypothesis with all the freedom that friendship, acquaintance and love naturally offer in life itself. Both stand outside religion, as formally understood; but sympathetically, as if longing at times to be inside, and sadly conscious of its insuperable intellectual difficulties. They are, so to speak, Christian fellow-travellers. How can omnipotence be just? How can omniscience be reconciled with free will? Such ancient and well-tried difficulties with the concept of the divine haunt their fictions, which remain essentially this-worldly, however, in their moral concerns, and never theological. The new novel, unlike the fictions of Tolkien and Lewis, is stubbornly secular, but with an ear cocked to the supernatural; it is no more anti-religious, that is to say, than Philip Larkin's poem 'Church Going', which intones sympathetically the values of an empty place where the dead lie buried and where prayer has once been valid. Iris Murdoch briefly warmed to Buddhism in her middle years, and more recently adopted a congenially fellow-travelling stance to Christianity much like Larkin's: 'There are advantages,' she has remarked in an interview, 'in staying with the icons of one's own people.' So the new novel is not a party to faith, only to a faintly envious sympathy with those who are faithful. Larkin, in his poem, had paused at the door of a village church to make sure there was nothing going on before modestly venturing in as a tourist.

Goodness is an intellectual search and enquiry, first and last, and not, as in the novel of earlier centuries, a reaffirmation of known truths. It is a seeking rather than a finding, and it ends with few certitudes. This is a fiction composed by university graduates – the first such school of fiction in English – and its primary emphasis, only remotely Cervantic, is on the dangers of false intellectualism and simplistic theories, and above all the arrogant notion that membership of an intelligentsia constitutes a credible claim to superior wisdom or superior virtue. The new hero, like Don Quixote, gets it wrong by study, but unlike Quixote he gets it right (more or less) by living, and he characteristically needs to educate himself by life after having partly de-educated himself through books. That is a pattern of fiction broadly like the world of Quixote or Mr Pickwick, but with the large ~~difference~~ that the new hero can change, and does. He unlearns the false learning of the schools by watching, listening and seeing; he is changed by life.

★   ★   ★

The campus novel – that highly characteristic invention of the 1950s in Anglo-America – provides a natural arena for that debate, since a university can easily represent a claim to false superiority, and such claims by their very nature cry out to be tested and explored. C. P. Snow's *The Masters* (1951) is a precursor rather than an instance: it tells a story of an election within a Cambridge college, a bitter tale of disappointed hopes; but it hardly questions the intellectual claims of academia, and it ultimately belongs, like other Snow novels, to a world of administrative ambitions where a university is seen as an out-of-town version of Whitehall. Promotion is everything there – easily more than love, power, sympathy, or sex. Such novels may not greatly dignify the world they describe, or even get it right; but their fascination with the inner workings of an administrative system are ultimately reverent, and Snow himself was to end his career in London and not in Cambridge, where he had begun as a scientist: a peer and, briefly, a government minister. Born in 1905, and publishing fiction in the 1930s, he belongs to another age.

Amis's *Lucky Jim* is something other; so is William Cooper's *Struggles of Albert Woods* (1952), written in slapstick vein by a follower of Snow's; so is Angus Wilson's *Anglo-Saxon Attitudes* (1956) and a fistful of novels soon after by David Lodge and Malcolm Bradbury, both of them professors of English in civic universities. Here the campus is king, and no breath of doubt is admitted that time spent at a university is the decisive influence on life, even if the claims of life take one willingly, even defiantly, out of universities forever. Bradbury's first novel, *Eating People is Wrong* (1959), tells what it felt like to be a first-generation student in a civic university like Leicester in the 1950s, puzzled and intrigued as a humble newcomer by liberal values of knowledge-for-its-own-sake and a wholly unfamiliar style of life. His friend David Lodge has explored the same theme in farcical vein in *Changing Places* (1975), *Small World* (1984) and *Nice Work* (1988), where farce is sophisticated by literary allusion and softened by the hint that humane values, however easily forgotten in the contest of fashion and the struggle for careers, may yet be of intrinsic worth. The point is made more seriously, and more savagely, in Bradbury's *The History Man* (1975), a fiercely partisan novel where an academic militant is exposed as a manipulative hypocrite, his ambitions directed more to sex and money than to revolution. Marxism can be a way to get rich or get laid. In the 1950s, in one fashion or another, academia suddenly looked important. Dons were no longer the comic derelicts that flit through Victorian fiction or the novels of Evelyn Waugh. They seek, and sometimes have, power. Their voices can carry around the world on radio or television, their printed utterances as prophet or pundit resound through newspapers and journals; their more reflected views to be memorialised, sage-like, on the bookshelf. Universities mark no mere rite of passage, now, between school and society. They are, at least potentially, places for creativity, power and prestige.

That sudden creativity has engendered its own literature. In a 1975 introduction to his first novel, *Jill*, Larkin has revealed what his college life in war-time Oxford was like, and how he first met Amis there – an account somewhat amended by Amis in his contribution to *Larkin at Sixty* (1982); and collections of essays with titles like *My Oxford* (1977) and *My Cambridge* (1977) have assembled reminiscences of how mind and character were once forged round and about the tender age of twenty. The campus novel has its theatrical equivalent, too, in the plays of Simon Gray, who went to Cambridge, and in *Jumpers* by Tom Stoppard, who went to no university at all. By the 1960s and 1970s, for a brief and intense phase, there was no greater theme in all fiction than this.

To understand why, the image of a tumbling wall might make a fitting emblem. Ivy-covered or not, universities had once protected themselves as if by walls from the outside gaze; effortlessly so, on the whole, since for centuries the world beyond had little curiosity about them, they cost the taxpayer nothing, and their inmates were proverbially remote and ineffectual. The new academic, by contrast, could be a creative artist, and he could dazzle the world as a poet, a dramatist or a novelist. He could also be a sage, TV-style, and an acclaimed public figure. The new campus novel is about such people, and by them: not just about dons but by dons. C. P. Snow had been a scientist at Christ's College, Cambridge before he turned to fiction; William Golding, a Salisbury schoolteacher who gave up teaching with the success of *Lord of the Flies*, has never exactly written an academic fiction, but *The Spire* (1964) is about the enclosed scholastic world of medieval architecture. These are older men. By the time *Lucky Jim* appeared, however, Amis was a lecturer in English at Swansea, though the novel is more likely to be based on recollections of a visit to his friend Larkin at Leicester, to whom it is dedicated; and Bradbury's *Eating People is*

Wrong was written by a graduate student at Manchester University. Iris Murdoch's prolific fiction touches only occasionally on academia; but she loves plots based on relations between teacher and pupil, master and disciple, and her interest in philosophy is so well known a fact that it informs any reading of her books, which are often felt to convey modern philosophical issues in lucid and digestible form. British universities can seldom afford the American luxury of Writers on Campus, but the ivy-clad wall can tumble from inwards, and in the 1950s it did. It is not that writers invaded universities. Academics became writers.

The hero of the campus novel, like his creator, often had one toe inside academia and the rest out. That is the fruitful ambiguity on which the new fiction was based. Lucky Jim abandons that life at the end of the book, forever convinced that its intellectual corruptions are subtler and deeper than those of money-making, and cheerfully enters the world of finance. The Lawrentian hero of A. Alvarez's first novel, *Hers* (1974), makes a broadly similar choice, selling off his hardbacks as a final gesture of abandonment; and when the hero of Michael Frayn's *The Trick of It* (1989) beds a lady whose writings have been the subject of his lectures and publications, he finds the experience amorously disappointing. All this smacks of disillusionment, though not exactly of regret. Academia is by now a necessary experience, in a manner it is never likely to have looked to Defoe or Dickens – something to be lived, for a time, and not forgotten – but quit in the consciousness that it is ultimately unlivable. That it should need to be exorcised in that fashion, however, or at all, still leaves it looking potent, richly formative and far from innocent, and the fiction that ultimately emerges from it is ex-academic in much the same sense that it is ex-socialist. Academia is to be savoured, even devoured, and then

transcended. There is a world elsewhere – usually
financial or literary London – and it is a world indeed in
the worldly sense, enticingly garnished with the gra-
tifications of the flesh and even the Devil. But one must
first sit and ponder, apparently, behind the ivy-covered
wall.

The borderline cases here are instructive. Philip Larkin spent his last years as a university librarian at Hull,
where he administered but did not teach; John Wain
resigned a lectureship at Reading to live in Oxford,
where he spent five years as a professor of poetry; Iris
Murdoch, though willingly leaving an Oxford teaching
post in her middle years, has lived there, or near it,
married to a professor; and David Lodge and Malcolm
Bradbury either retired early or went part-time. Some
toes, evidently, may be left in the water. But all that is to
characterise rather than to explain, and the lofty prestige
of universities in the post-war world remains a phenomenon that has still to be convincingly analysed.
Their influence on fiction, immense as it has been, is
evidently only part of a larger pattern of social influence.
Some day the theme may find its historian, who will
find many taxing questions to answer. Why, for example, did the author of *Lucky Jim* wait for nearly ten years
before following his own hero to the metropolis? Literature sometimes gets ahead of life, but with realistic
fiction one wonders how it can.

★   ★   ★

The search for goodness could take the new hero into
academia and out again, despairing of its false intellectualism and its established assumption that to be intelligent is only and always to be an intellectual. In that
severely limited sense, and only in that, the new anti-
Modernism was anti-intellectual. It hated pretension,

however, because it loved the life of mind; and what
Golding once called a 'blow for the ordinary universe' is
a denial, often explicit, of a pre-war tradition of fiction
composed for an intelligentsia and self-consciously excluding the vulgar appeals of fast-paced narrative and
clarity of assertion. There, at least, the new novelists –
secular though they were – and Christian revivalists like
Tolkien were altogether at one; and *Lord of the Flies* and
The Lord of the Rings, which coincidentally appeared in
the same year, share that large element in common.
They are equally a protest against Bloomsbury and
Modernism, against novels without narrative momentum, incidents unbased on a shared knowledge of a
familiar and engrossing world, and analysis without
moral commitment.

The ordinary universe is a social manifesto as well as a
literary position. *Under the Net* ends with its drifting hero
finding work; *Lucky Jim* with marriage and a job. The
love of money, then, is not (as one was told) the root of
all evil. Mankind seeks status even more avidly than
wealth, and more self-corruptingly; and intellectual
affectation can be a darker sin than whatever vulgarities
arise out of a simple greed for gain. Samuel Johnson,
who was something of a hero of the new school, once
remarked that a man is seldom so innocently employed
as when he is making money, and that celebrated
remark might serve as a slogan for much of modern
British fiction. Whatever is the matter with British life, it
is not materialism. If only it were ... A man might be
more virtuous if more selfish, after all, as more than one
eighteenth-century moralist proposed, and more generous if he had more to be generous with.

Behind the new anti-Modernism flits the shadow of
that old anti-Modernist D. H. Lawrence. Lawrence died
in 1930, but his mounting vogue in the decade or two
after his death, not least in universities, had kept a flame

of thoughtful anti-Modernism alive. Larkin has told
how Lawrence was one of his favourite novelists when
he was young, along with Isherwood, Maugham and
Waugh,[22] and many in and after the Second World War
were to ponder the strange, radical genius of famed
humility of social origin and ambiguous political stance
who had helped keep the realistic spirit alive and potent
in an age when its intellectual prestige stood low. 'A
work must enact its own meaning' and 'Never trust the
teller, trust the tale' – such Lawrentian tags, garbled as
they may have been from the writings of the Master,
could inspire and cheer the literate young of the 1940s.
Lawrence's rising reputation in the years after his death
made the critical shift back to realism easier. 'It was as if
a key turned,' Margaret Drabble once remarked of her
easy transition from student days at Cambridge to the
life of an instant bestseller in realistic fiction with her
first novel, *A Summer Birdcage* (1962). Between the world
wars that tradition had thinned. But its thread since
Defoe is unbroken, and it is the absence of any break in
a national tradition now nearly three centuries long that
helps to make it effortless. Realism is a technique which,
being known from childhood reading, never needs to be
consciously studied, and certainly the effort required to
compose a corpus of novels, like the noteworthy succession of Anita Brookner romances that began with *A Start
in Life* (1981), is always more likely to be emotional than
technical. Realism, though humanly exacting, is technically what comes naturally. The analysis of a remembered life, after all, or of the life around one, is continuous with living itself: with gossip heard and overheard, with unspoken thoughts, with watching and
listening to friends or strangers. If realism can break
your heart, as Salman Rushdie remarked, it comes easily
in every other sense. It can arise from talk overheard on
the top of a bus, or anywhere. No one who reads such

books can doubt that they are composed by those who find novel-writing, in the most flattering sense of the word, easy: the sheer fertility of the school forbids any other interpretation. Such books are commonly fast-written and substantially unrevised. It is the ultimate paradox of this highly academic school of fiction that it defies all the usual rules of academic scrupulosity, as if fiction were a breaking-out, a holiday from cares. But then Lawrence, too, one of the first university-trained novelists in the language, had not behaved otherwise.

★   ★   ★

The new realists proclaimed two large truths about the world, the one severely literary and the other not.

The literary truth is that Modernism was in the end a starved and blighted world, joylessly based on a denial that language can depict the real. That was its challenge. But as the new realists and the Christian revivalists equally understood, mankind needs its shared experience of reality; and conversation apart, it is doubtful if anything but fiction can do it as well, or do it at all. Modernists never wrote stories, as that word is commonly understood, and to all public appearances they seldom read them. 'I am unable to be confident from Mr. Eliot's writings,' Iris Murdoch once reproachfully wrote in a theoretical defence of realism, 'that he has ever enjoyed and admired any novel.'[23] The remark, if not strictly accurate, is profoundly just in a general sense. Modernism seldom speaks of a shared experience. It refuses to tell; it even denies, in its extreme theorising moods, that there is anything certain to be told. Eliot's *Four Quartets*, like Pound's *Cantos*, alternate dizzyingly between the sceptical and the dogmatic, and by the 1950s that paradox had come to look insoluble. If intellectualism only leads to a cultivated despair or a hankering after dictatorship, then it is time to give ordinary intelligence a chance.

The new fiction tells of a world its readers live. Accuracy, which is first and last its claim to existence, has many aspects, of which the simplest is mimicry; and Kingsley Amis happens, not coincidentally, to be a notable mimic in conversation. Realism is an extended version of that conversational gift: it mimicks the real world. In British terms that means reflecting the multifarious ways in which speech and gesture reveal or seek to conceal social status and social pretension: and in a fast-shifting, highly unrigid world like the British, status is far more often a matter of pretension than of birth. Like Shaw's Eliza in *Pygmalion*, you are what you decide to be, more or less; and no people on earth, one may suspect, is so adept at jumping hierarchies by efficiently switching accent or style. Self-promotion of that sort may be a matter for amused comment, but it is widely accepted that one may choose one's place in the pecking order, or try to, and that in Britain parentage does not irreversibly define class. 'Look, I know it's a dodgy topic,' some one remarks in Amis's *Stanley and the Women* (1984), 'but you are lower class, aren't you, darling?'; to which the admirably candid reply is:

> I was before I came up in the world, true, but lower-middle-class, not working-class. Very important distinction. My old dad got really wild if you said he was working-class. Worse than calling him a Jew,

which sounds as if parentage counts, but not to the point where it counts for everything. And no one is stuck with it unless he wants to be.

Class accents lie at the heart of such mimicry, though on the printed page a betraying turn of phrase, or a tell-tale choice of words like 'dodgy' or 'darling', can be represented more easily than an impure vowel. Such differences are not a distinguishing truth of British life, merely a truth. France, Germany and the United States have them too: in fact it is a question whether any large language-system is without them. Vocabulary and articulation often reflect social standing in Britain, to be sure: but where do they not? It would be more surprising if it were otherwise – or so the new novel seems to tell, or remind. Since dress, gait and table manners instantly distinguish social rank, all over the world, why not speech as well? People need to be told these things, after all, and without asking, so that a few clear social indicators are a simple necessity in life and not, in themselves, a matter for regret. Language, in any case, is often the subtlest indicator that there is: much better than clothes, since one can daily or hourly change one's clothes. The fertile play of dialogue in these novels, often predominating on the printed page, is a constant stream of signals flashed to the reader to help him estimate the age, the mood, and the standing – real or pretended – of their characters from instant to instant. These are status-hungry beings eager to define a place in the world for themselves and for others.

To perceive that fiction can describe a known and shared experience – to accept, in effect, the chief claim of realism – is to perceive that, in the end, no single or simple doctrine, whether Marxist, Christian or other, can do the whole job. 'This doesn't apply,' as the teenage Amis remarked in his army barracks, abandoning Marxism because it failed to fit the real world. You cannot, in a post-industrial nation, make more than fitful sense of an early Victorian doctrine of class-war. Hence the pull of tolerance. Realism signifies a love, or at least an acceptance, of diversity. In his second novel, *The Inheritors*, Golding has stood so far back from modern historical progress as to imagine the supersession of innocent, hairy Neanderthalers by 'bone-face men' in a prehistoric age: they wear clothes or, as the primitive eye sees it, they step outside their skins. No shared knowledge there, but an imaginative leap that stretches realism to the farthest point and yet preserves its characteristic obsession with speech and gesture. The realistic novelist's world is a roomy one, large in space and time. As Iris Murdoch has remarked in admiration of Dickens and Tolstoy,[24] the great novelist creates a house fit for free character to live in: free, that is, to live lives untrammelled by the allegorical or the stereotypic- al, to be as quirky, unpredictable, and self-contradicting as beings one knows in a real world.

The stream of novels that followed the coronation of realism in 1953 may in all likelihood have proved even wider, in scope and tolerance, than the founders of the school ever dared to hope or to expect. Its polarities are form and language: Muriel Spark the mistress of form, her designs tightly, even constrictively imposed; Anthony Burgess of language, a successor (perhaps because of his Irish ancestry) of Joyce. Paul Scott's *Raj Quartet*, a fictional foursome collected in 1976 and with the pendant of a fifth novel, *Staying On* (1977), is a vast canvas devoted to the transfer of power in India and its sequel: too close in time to be seen, altogether clearly, as historical fiction, too distant in place to be a shared world; though like E. M. Forster before him, Scott chose an alien sun to define the outlines and shadows of the English abroad, where their habits of mind look all the sharper, odder and more endearing against the back- ground of an exotic land. Anita Brookner's novels are London-based, and they revive in their concise and elegant style, in fictions at once grim and yet subtly self-mocking, the Brontëan theme of lonely, loving heroines more sensitive than beautiful – 'she was attrac- tive enough for a clever woman, but it was principally as a clever woman that she was attractive' – and, as in the Brontës, without the solace of a happy ending. They teach the bitter truth that in the life of a great city one needs others and yet is always alone. Such a vision is as microscopic as Paul Scott's is panoramic; and a future historian, reading the *Raj Quartet* or J. G. Farrell's *Siege of Krishnapur* (1973), which tells of the Indian Mutiny, might easily make the mistake of supposing that the British are nostalgic for lost empire. That would be a misunderstanding. As Kipling complained, they hardly noticed it when it was there; and since its conversion into a Commonwealth of Nations in 1947, with Indian independence, they have hardly noticed that a Commonwealth is not the same thing. The attraction of India is not the breadth and scope of the imperial idea but the sniff of a richly coherent world that novelists rightly value as the supreme end of fiction. As Graham Greene once created a Greene-land, habitable only by creatures distinctive of his mind, so do novelists since his day seek a setting that holds together, and one that gives character a space to breathe and act in. That setting can be imperial India or a lonely flat in a great city haunted by thoughts of lost love. Either way, it is a coherent world to be defined and explained, at once like and unlike the world that readers know.

If tolerance is essential to such fiction, then the novelist tolerates, even if he does not defend or excuse, much that is outside the range of other arts, not excluding affectation, pretension, self-contradiction and sin: 'among the Filthy, filthy'. This is a secular world, in its emphases, even if some of its novelists like Barbara Pym and A. N. Wilson have been dedicatedly Christian. It is not religion that drives it, or theory; and the rejection of Marxism now looks, in retrospect, like an inevitable part of its natural growth. Whatever novelists may believe about the universe, they do not demand of their readers a formal belief in God or the Devil, or in the forces of history, and the tolerances they expect are wide. Amis's *Stanley and the Women* drew blood, for a time, from feminist opinion, and is said to have been blocked for a period from entry into the United States; and Salman Rushdie's *Satanic Verses* (1988) forced its author, a Muslim-born Indian, into hiding in 1989 for its alleged blasphemy against the Prophet. But such incidents are wildly exceptional, and based on fanatical misunderstandings of what fiction does or seeks to do. Realism educates slowly and by stages, teaching how to alter a world rather than transform it. It is in its nature neither conservative nor iconoclastic. Amis's *The Old Devils* (1986) is a withering portrait of ageing desire, a theme seldom treated in literature since Shakespeare's sonnets; but its final message is one of pity. If some of these novels, like Iris Murdoch's *The Bell* (1958), stand tiptoe at the door of faith, they are content to remain there and not to enter in, at least as worshippers. They offer hope rather than salvation, consolation rather than cure, reform rather than revolution. They are prudent. The world is what it is, and will remain so; and you learn to live within it by adjusting yourself rather than it. No wonder Anthony Powell called one of his novels *The Acceptance World* (1955). The hero of such books does not submit. But he adapts, not without pain; and even the most romantic heroine learns to accept, like the heroine of Anita Brookner's *Providence* (1982), that her lover was after all bound in the end to prefer another.

The learning theme is classic. In Greek tragedy, in most of Jane Austen's novels, a leading figure in the drama realises with a sense of shock that the world is other than once imagined, and accepts that it is so. Such fictions are about recognition. Realism hardly admits of simple recognitions, Greek-style, and in the diversity of social life there is unlikely to be a single moment when, as in a religious ecstasy, life is seen as a whole. Modern fiction deals rather in the partial illuminations of the moment. Life can dazzle with its sensuality, its colour, its sheer abundance of choice. And in the end it offers not one way, as the ideologue or the mystic would claim, but rather an acceptance that diversity is forever a fact of life. Instead of choosing one road or another, like Hercules at the crossroads – sin or virtue, company or solitude, capitalism or collectivism – as ancient religions and modern dogmas have sometimes demanded, it invites one rather to settle into a questioning and critical acceptance of things as they are. Most reality, after all, is beyond understanding. 'What puzzles me', someone remarks of her new kittens at the close of *Under the Net*, 'is why those two should be pure Siamese and the other ones quite different, instead of their all being half tabby and half Siamese.' And to that ultimate challenge of the book the hero cannot reply, except by realising that he does not know the answer, and that he is glad he does not know. For all theories, in the end, cheapen and despoil. 'I don't know why it is,' he finally admits. 'It's just one of the wonders of the world.'

5

A Critical Moment

For some twenty years after the ending of the war, in 1945, literary criticism was a dominating force in the Anglo-American literary mind.

It was as if a bit player had become a star, a menial suddenly promoted into the centre of things. Something comparable, and no less surprising, had happened a century earlier with the art-criticism of John Ruskin, and there is often something unnerving in the spectacle of an activity once thought of as specialist and tedious catapulted into sudden acclaim. The effects, though short-lived, were astounding. For the length of an entire generation, literary criticism profoundly affected the creativity, even the morality, of the age. It changed how people lived as well as how they thought: a sort of secular church, so to speak, and like many churches a hotbed of internecine sects. It provided, too, intellectual drama. Post-war criticism was 'gladiatorial', as John Wain remarked years later, in 1972, when the excitement had died down; and attractive to the young for just that reason, since the young feed on moral drama: 'they need to feel that they are proving themselves by bravely attacking something powerful.'[1] There never had been such a moment, for critics; there has never been such a moment since.

Literary criticism, it is easy to forget, is a kind of literature as well as a kind of criticism, and some of the best prose of the post-war years belongs to the journals and critical collections of the age. It is not a wholly secondary activity. It is also, simply because it is critical, a sort of potential morality – even an actual one – and no one can understand the Age of Criticism without grasping that, like the Crusades or the Reformation, its prime purpose was a far-reaching reform of the human spirit. No missionary was ever more dedicated than this. When it ended in the mid 1960s, to be replaced in quick succession by sociology, anthropology, and linguistic theory, it turned introspective in its defeat, wasting its energies on the grimly unavailing task of seeking, and never finding, a theoretical basis for what it did or had once done. The critical theories that engaged the 1970s, however, are no part of this story, except as an epilogue is part of an epic. They belong to an era of withdrawal, when criticism turned inward and ceased, out of self-doubt, to address any world beyond itself. That was not the mood of the 1950s, when critics held sway far outside universities and learned journals, and knew it. The retreat led by theorists was of a dwindling army that felt itself to be beaten, and at best it could only remember its victories. But the claim to criticise the world through its literary culture, in its day, had been little short of a claim to rule that culture and that world.

The phrase 'The Age of Criticism' seems to have been the invention of the American poet Randall Jarrell; and like the Enlightenment, and some other dignified terms of intellectual history, it began as something like a term of dismissal. There was always something faintly implausible, on either side of the Atlantic, about confusing a critic with a great man. Perhaps that is why the age was shortlived. The fame of Lionel Trilling in New York, of F. R. Leavis in Cambridge, peaked in the years after 1945, in their middle age, and their consciousness of fame and influence reached its climax in the early 1950s with the appearance of two essay-collections, Trilling's *The Liberal Imagination* (1950) and Leavis's *The Common Pursuit* (1952). Such books are essentially collections of moral tracts. But they emerged out of an analytical fervour: the practice of stylistic analysis pioneered in Cambridge before the war by I. A. Richards and his pupil William Empson. The mood of that enquiry was romantically scientific, so to speak, impelled by a search for technicality based on a confident assumption that science had provided the arts with a lasting model of analytical objectivity. Impressionism was out: henceforth, it was felt, the study of literature must emulate the natural sciences if it was to hope to survive as worthy of any dignity and respect.

Practical criticism, Cambridge-style, crossed the Atlantic in the 1940s and returned after 1945 under the name of the American New Criticism; to be emulated in 1955 in *Interpretations*, a collection of analytical essays by various hands edited by John Wain. Four years earlier F. W. Bateson of Oxford had founded *Essays in Criticism*, a quarterly meant to emulate or surpass Leavis's *Scrutiny* (1932–53), then nearing its natural end. By the early 1950s the riot was on. To be new was to be critical. To be conservative, intellectually speaking, was to be uncritical – immune to American academic influences, unanalytical, culpably cosy. The lines were drawn, the terms of a new moral drama, as gladiatorial as any boat-race or general election, were widely accepted and understood. 'I believe in criticism' was a slogan to gather a coterie and even a crowd.

The claim that literary criticism can influence life, if you let it, or even transform it, is not in itself absurd. Nor is the claim that you should let it. Some of the larger literary claims made by the New Critics of the 1950s, by contrast, are to be quoted now only to indicate a mood forever lost. Critical analysis, one student journal proclaimed, 'generally produces results more significant than the best creative work now being written,' a judgement offered not as a complaint but as a boast:

As the inventor of the most complete terminology of the creative process, the critic, borrowing his methods from the logician as well as from the psychologist, has replaced the metaphysician, since his findings show with a greater exactitude the nature of what we are.[2]

That confusion between terminology and rigour, truth and exactitude, was to prove a weakness to the New Criticism in later years, since it laid on the critic a continuous duty to adopt or devise terms rigorous enough to satisfy himself and others. It coexisted with an ardently self-purifying ethos, where every emotion in literature and life was to be tried and tested against moral examples offered by the great poets and novelists of past time: by Blake's *Songs of Innocence and Experience*, by George Eliot's *Middlemarch*, by the fiction (above all) of D. H. Lawrence. The important thing, as John Wain was to put it years later in 'The Vanishing Critic', looking back wonderingly over a good quarter-century at his own vanished youth, was 'to respond to life with one's emotional priorities in the right order.' In other ages that had been the task of the Church, and it is hardly an exaggeration to say that, for some in the 1950s, criticism was an organised religion. A belief in criticism was an affirmation to be made in earnest assemblies of like minds.

The morality of the critical moment is more interesting, in the end, than its techniques, and that interest may prove abiding. The literary intelligence at work in the best post-war critical journals still looks as arresting, in its moral urgency, as Ruskin's *Modern Painters* or the essays of Matthew Arnold or George Eliot. This was an embattled and a battling faith. A battle needs two sides, and the New Critics quickly found an enemy in the bland Sunday reviewing of Harold Nicolson, that elegant survivor of a politer age, or in the amiable and

harmless writings of Lord David Cecil. The New Critic,
by reaction, liked to look tough. 'I have been waiting for
a long time to get my hands on this one', a review of
Nicolson by Kingsley Amis began. The book was called
Good Behaviour (1955), and no doubt the very title was an
incitement. By then the conventional restraints of courtesy were felt to have had their day, and outlived it: the
New Critic was above all a rebel, even a terrorist.

The position of the New Criticism needs to be put in
focus. Its moral claims were, in the most literal sense of
the word, conservative, in that it enjoined ancient truths
and established values, and Samuel Johnson as well as
William Blake was a hero. All that could easily coexist
with political and religious radicalism, and in William
Empson it did. Born in 1906, he was eleven years
younger than Leavis but far more precocious, and spent
his early teaching life, as a pupil and disciple of his
Cambridge mentor I. A. Richards, in the Far East. When
he finally returned to England in 1952, an unrecon-
structed radical from the 1930s, he was appalled to
discover that an acquiescent temper of mind, even
Christianity itself, had returned to haunt a literary world
he had once supposed forever cleared of the religious
taint. His mounting literary reputation was by then
sustained by poems as well as criticism, though he had
abandoned the writing of poems before the war: 'It
struck me they were bad,' he told an interviewer years
later, 'I didn't want to print them'[3]; so that though his
Collected Poems (1955) were a minor intellectual sensation
when they finally appeared, they belong to another
time. For the last forty years and more of his life, down
to his death in 1984, Empson wrote almost nothing but
prose.

His first post-war book, *The Structure of Complex Words*
(1951), combines a lexical passion for the history of
words with a free-wheeling fascination with literary

Freudianism. But it is still a work of analysis, not of dogmatics. *Milton's God* (1961), by contrast, represents a coming-out: it is a dogmatic work with no holds barred. It is the only continuous book he ever wrote after 1945 – the rest is all essays and articles – and perhaps the only entire book by any British-born critic of the age to work moral and literary concerns into a single exercise of radical intellect, as indifferent to tact as to fashion and concerned only with truth itself. Once mistaken for a joker, he could henceforth be seen as a crank: an important advance in reputation, though this playful and darting mind was seldom so serious as when it was spoofing, or so earnest in intent as when making a joke. The comic, in his contention, is what in literature is above all else revealing. Poetry, he once wrote as an undergraduate, 'is written with the sort of joke you find in hymns'.[4] Most people have never noticed that there are any jokes in hymns, so that the point is characteristically mind-stretching. A talent, it is said, hits a target: a genius hits something you did not even know was there. Empson's criticism never looked merely talented, and it hit something you did not know was there.

It was a mind unique, too, among British critics of the age in possessing a world-view wholly peculiar to itself. Few critics bother to have a theory of history, unless a borrowed one. Empson's was his own. Variously influenced in youth by Freud and Marx, by Richards and T. S. Eliot, he emerged defiant of his sources to adopt a view of civilisation which, by the time he came to write *Milton's God*, was fiercely and outrageously his own. This is criticism as original thought. Humankind, to summarise, has been moving shoddywards since about 480 BC, when Confucius, Buddha, the Second Isaiah and Pythagoras died: to be succeeded, sages of wisdom and toleration that they were, by a return to superstition not unlike the reactions that tragically followed the

Enlightenment or Victorian rationalism. Monotheism, for Empson, is the arch-villain of human history and the prime source of intolerance, and it is a villain of irrepressible energy: first the Judaic revival, then the foundation of Christianity, then Islam. No wonder Milton was aware that the ways of God needed more justifying than even the greatest of English epics could contrive to do; and *Paradise Lost*, as Empson believed, is a poem more than occasionally conscious of the ultimate injustice of the dogma of atonement, and it thrives poetically on its contradictions. Ambiguity is no longer a verbal device to be lexically explored, by the 1950s, but a self-lacerating truth of the poet's mind. This was to stake a large claim to moral originality, and it is a work that has earned the right to be revered and detested. Like the writings of Johnson and Coleridge it raises the possibility that criticism can be serious, in the sense of making a lasting difference to conviction. *Milton's God* was Empson's last book, in his lifetime, though when he died he was collecting at least three others: *Using Biography* (1984), on Marvell, Dryden, Fielding, Yeats, Eliot and Joyce; *Essays on Shakespeare* (1986); and a book of Renaissance essays, as well as a massive ragbag (as he called it) of papers and reviews dating back to the 1920s which, when it posthumously appeared as *Argufying* (1987), was rapidly seen by many to be the finest critical miscellany in the language.

Empson's criticism bespeaks a man of some social rank, and in manner it is appropriately insouciant and grand. This is radicalism at its most aristocratic. He seldom troubles to verify a reference or document a case, his rejections tend to be magisterially dismissive, his judgements readily upstage even his most august victims. He once reproached Sir Philip Sidney for his famous refusal of a cup of water on a Dutch battlefield as an act that looks 'aggressively holy', and it is hard to imagine any other critic of the age allowing himself such a remark, or even conceiving of it: 'The okay thing would be to drink some of the cup himself and pass it on, leaving most of it to the other man...'[5] There survives a long and highly circumstantial account of his conversation with the Queen when he was newly a professor at Sheffield,[6] and one is seldom in doubt that this is one who has moved among the great, and without strain. All that is essential to his critical insouciance. To criticise, in this vein, is to forget reverence and argufy; it is also, for Empson, to fantasise. His favourite verb-form is 'would have been' and 'would have thought', and he shows an endless propensity to turn everything – Shakespeare's sonnets, Marvell's supposed marriage, the autobiographical subtext to Joyce's *Ulysses* – into a story, and usually a rather good story. That happy and wholly characteristic confusion of fact and supposition makes his criticism as readable, at times, as an eccentric novel by a country gentleman more at ease at a hunt-ball than in a classroom, at a levée than in a seminar.

Empson was not a scholar, and hardly wished to be one, though he respected scholarship – especially the kind that had once produced the *Oxford English Dictionary* to provide others with a godsent place to start a critical argument. No doubt there is something mildly shocking about such behaviour, academically considered, though on a long view *The Structure of Complex Words* may look like the most sustained compliment ever paid by a critical mind to a great dictionary. Nor was he anything of a theorist, and hardly troubled to read much of the new wave of 'bother-headed' critics, as he called them, spawned by the 1960s. He saw things in a flash and put them down in a sentence or at most a paragraph. In his post-war writings authorial intention, banished to the servants' quarters by Richards and the

American New Criticism, was restored to a dignity it should never have lost; and his abandonment of discipleship to Richards now looks with hindsight both belated and inevitable. Few geniuses seems so untouched, in a fashion-ridden world, by the fashions of the moment. His ferocious anti-Christianity, in no way the creature of fashion, never waned even in old age; and he never forgot that literature is about something, and that it matters whether that something is true or false. His largest fault, perhaps, and one natural to a good hater, was a congenital inability to accept that mortal creatures hold incompatible views and behave in ways incompatible with their views, so that to the end of his days he declined to accept any difference between holding a speculative opinion that is evil and being bad. That intransigence, though ultimately unrealistic, remains impressive in its obstinacy. 'A man who believes in Hell,' he once wrote, 'can't help relating the prospect of it to his feelings about life in general'.[7] It is a remark that engagingly suggests how little, as a devout atheist, he understood the relation between religion and life. Most believers, it is likely, find it difficult much of the time even to remember what it is they are supposed to believe.

★   ★   ★

The reversion of criticism, at least in academies, from practice to theory after the demise of *Scrutiny* in 1953 and the appearance of Empson's last lifetime book in 1961 was perhaps something to be expected, as failures of nerve often follow phases of confidence and excess. It is also regrettable. With the revival of theory, criticism lost the greater part of its contact with English, with literature, and with England itself. Theory was no longer a drawing-room activity, as in the eighteenth century. It was now, by its nature, an international enquiry, like the physical sciences. There is no distinctive British contribution, and can be none. A set of dogmas borrowed from Paris in the 1960s and earnestly debated in international conferences has no national existence, and seeks none. Perhaps Peter Fuller's *Theoria* (1988), a call for a return to earnest Ruskinian values by a critic who had lost his faith in Modernism, contrives to be theoretical and distinctively British at the same time; but that is the work of an art critic.

The loss of critical nerve, though widespread, was never general. It can be charted in the rise and fall of journals which, as early as the 1950s, moved from severely literary concerns into a mixture of politics, the fine arts and travelogue. Cyril Connolly's quarterly *Horizon* died in December 1949, after a ten-year run: the very type of the pure literary review, but unable to thrive, apparently, in austerity Britain. Connolly's famous valedictory – 'It is closing time in the gardens of the West' – may be little more than the self-excusing of an indolent man, but what replaced *Horizon* (1940–50) and *Penguin New Writing* (1940–50) was something far brisker and far less mandarin. *Encounter* was launched in London in 1953, an Anglo-American monthly whose appeal was always international, and above all intellectually anti-communist; and the *London Magazine* started in the following year, first under the editorship of John Lehmann, then of Alan Ross – a general magazine where literature is no more than one concern among others. There was no place in the new Elizabethan era, apparently, outside universities, for a specifically literary journal mainly concerned with the Condition of England. Even *TLS*, which momentously abandoned the anonymity of its book-reviews in 1974 under the editorship of John Gross, is cosmopolitan and more-than-literary in its range; and its newer rival the *London*

Review of Books, begun in 1979 with Karl Miller as editor, was a fortnightly avowedly conducted in imitation of the *New York Review of Books*: both of them, as it happens, Anglo-American and more in their choice of authors and topics. Compared with pre-war journals like *John O'London's Weekly*, this is a highly anti-insular and anti-cosy world. Ideas, as everyone knows, have no frontiers. But literatures sometimes do, and these are journals that have chosen to dedicate themselves to ideas. That guarantees a certain deliberate power to disturb. There are bedside books but no bedside ideas; and books, plays and films are now assumed to exist less to amuse or console than to stimulate and provoke.

★   ★   ★

The Condition of England, for all that, remains a question in the wider critical polemics of the age. Both F. R. Leavis and C. S. Lewis, for example, though dogmatic opposites and even rivals, believed in Englishness, though Lewis was a Belfast man and Leavis mistakenly supposed, by some, to be Jewish. When Lewis moved his teaching from Oxford to Cambridge in 1954, for the last nine years of his life, the drama of that confrontation was somewhat intensified, and it was not always noticed in the heat of debate how much they shared. Both were essayists rather than scholars, belonging to an age before English studies had accumulated its own technical machinery; so that their freedom to polemicise about past centuries now looks, in retrospect, like a liberty lost. Both saw English literature as the expression of a nation, and had little truck with foreign theorising. Both were rootedly masculine in their view of life; both ardent moralists; both, as sages, contrived to attract a following that could be independent of all considerations of religion and politics. That Leavis was secular and Lewis Christian matters less, on a long view, than one might expect. Lewis's *Allegory of Love* (1936), the book that made him known, was almost all written while he was still an atheist; and his Christian polemics, which began as war-time broadcasts, never prevented him from winning secular admirers. Nor did his pervasive conservatism of mind repel radicals in any altogether reliable way. Leavis, a radical socialist before 1950, turned briefly liberal before adopting in his last years a bitterly conservative stance that favoured no party of state, hating economic growth and the European Community, so that long before his death in 1978 his idealism had been soured by the varied spectacle of human folly; but though always outside religion, he was in no way hostile to it, and admired its moral seriousness. The differences, then, were supremely literary.

Both, too, were good writers. Leavis's reputation as a crabbed stylist and boldly innovative thinker who had been rejected by a university where he spent his entire life was largely a figment of his own mind, and so much of his post-war life was devoted to mythologising his own career that it is difficult, by now, to recognise what a conventional figure in his place and day he always was. A devotion to T. S. Eliot was commonplace, almost compulsory, in Cambridge literary circles in the 1930s and 1940s; a devotion to D. H. Lawrence only mildly less so. Seen in his context, which was inter-war Cambridge, Leavis was never much of an innovator, and it is hard to see his critical notoriety, which reached its apogee in the 1950s and early 1960s, as anything other than a triumph of style. His claim to persecution, sincere as it was, was an invention, and no other critic has made of his own stigmata the stuff of critical debate. 'For the first half-dozen years of *Scrutiny* I had no post and no salary, and was hard put to it to make a living,' he once wrote in characteristic vein.[8] In fact his university post followed the foundation of *Scrutiny* by only four years, in 1936, and his college fellowship too; he always, unlike most of his colleagues, had a private income; and his birth and upbringing, as the son of a prosperous trades-man, was well up to average and perhaps a little above. His career was privileged beyond Lewis's, as recounted in his memoir *Surprised by Joy* (1955): no trauma of pre-1914 boarding schools, no fighting on the Western front (only ambulance work), no pecuniary struggle to survive. But his pose as a victim of a harsh literary establishment was utterly essential to his own sense of being and to a craving for young disciples; for unlike Lewis he seldom enjoyed, for long, or sought to enjoy, the friendship of his contemporaries.

As myths go, the Leavis myth was widely successful: but then what teacher, when he tells the young that he has been ill-treated by the world for his opinions, is not believed? An early collaborator, late in his career, re-vealed to an astonished world that, in his first writings Leavis had fabricated evidence as quotations.[9] That contrasts wildly with his reputation, which was that of a fearless truth-teller, and one of his post-war disciples has told how Leavis's convictions about the 'mecha-nised vulgarity' of industrialism so possessed his youth-ful consciousness that its abandonment amounted to 'a personal crisis lasting several years.'[10] This sounds like the more-than-religious intensity of a man without religion. But like other religions, Leavism offered the sweet joys of antagonism. As Donald Davie has re-marked, his concept of a minority culture was modelled on the 'gathered church' of the Dissenters – a commun-ion of saints – and the irreplaceable charm of *Scrutiny* to the post-war undergraduate lay ultimately in the simple fact that on every issue it made things look simple: 'a present of perhaps a dozen authors or books or whole periods and genres of literature which I not only *need* not but *should not* read.'[11] This was a radicalism that asked little, in practical terms, of its adherents: in fact life became pleasanter and easier. A future director of the National Theatre who admired Leavis's lectures at Cambridge has since remarked that 'all we students pretended we sped to his lectures to imbibe his humanism,' whereas in fact they were enjoying his character-assassinations: 'Strange that a great moralist should be so destructive about creative artists.'[12] Not so strange, perhaps if one reflects that all moral dramas need villains as well as heroes, and that Leavis above all offered moral drama. When he attacked C. P. Snow in *Two Cultures?* (1962), it was the last act of a drama in which he had played for thirty years. Drama is a set of oppositions. 'The great English novelists are Jane Austen, George Eliot, Henry James and Joseph Conrad,' Leavis's *Great Tradition* (1948) authoritatively began. Dramatic oppositions can be between good and bad or, more subtly, between good and good. Leavis always laid claim to the subtler view of controversy, but his doctrine was always easily open, as he knew, to cruder interpretations, and the fire-and-brimstone of his prose sometimes made it hard to interpret or understand in any other way. 'Critics have found me narrow,' his opening paragraph continues, 'and I have no doubt that my opening proposition, whatever I may say to explain and justify it, will be adduced in reinforcement of their strictures,' adding bitterly that 'the only way to escape misrepresentation is never to ... *say* anything.' That gambit illustrates Leavis's magisterial grasp of polemical style, and it succeeds at once in looking bold and in insinuating craftily. 'Critics have found me narrow' implies that his reputation is already controversial, a truth of which he was justly proud, and it is a provocation aptly calculated to make one read on; and to claim that the only way to escape misrepresentation is to say nothing implies that something momentous is about to be said, that it is his habit and custom to do so, and that he is widely hated because he does. These are attention-getting claims, skilfully imparted, and they represent a growing contrast between Leavis and Lewis. Where Lewis looked at the world around him, even when he was writing autobiography, Leavis looked ever more attentively at himself. 'He should have called his paper "Why I am a great critic",' a disciple sadly remarked on leaving one of his seminars. In the long wake of a critical career that had begun in the 1930s avowedly in imitation of Richards and Empson and which ended with his death at the age of 83, his final achievement of style was above all to create, for a time, a compelling image of himself. And no one who writes badly ever succeeded in doing that.

Lewis's self-image, though less carefully cultivated, has lasted longer in the English-speaking world at large, and even swollen since his death, which was in 1963, into something of a cult. He is even the subject of a play. Some of the reasons are religious; some literary; some to do with his well-merited reputation as a blunt-talking character who, like Samuel Johnson, drew the wisdom of his conversation and letters from ancient sources, Christian or pagan, as much as modern – a wisdom somehow as congenial to the sceptical as to the godly. Oddly enough, his criticism gives off less of a religious odour than that of Leavis, who was secular all his thinking life. It is Leavis rather than Lewis who, when he writes of literature, sounds washed in the blood of the Lamb. Leavis's *Great Tradition* is headed by a motto from a letter of D. H. Lawrence declaring that writing makes him feel as if he 'stood naked for the fire of Almighty God to go through me.' Spilt religion, all too clearly, can be more intense than the real thing, and Lewis was always far too much of an Enlightenment

man for talk like that. It would have embarrassed him,
even sickened him. He largely avoided the novels of
Lawrence, as a theme, and found such enthusiasm even
in the act of religious worship both perilous and extravagant. 'Leavis demands moral earnestness: I prefer
morality,' he once told Kingsley Amis in a characteristically Johnsonian antithesis, adding that he would sooner live among people who did not cheat at cards than
among the sort who are earnest about not cheating.[13]
The classical spirit in which he was trained never lost its
hold upon him; the spirit of the pagan authors he
revered in their original languages coexisted in his mind
with an Anglicanism more committed in substance than
fervent in style; and as the new novel of the 1950s
revived the techniques of eighteenth-century fiction, so
did Lewis's critical prose revive the world of hard-
hitting supper-party debates that Boswell records. His
early defence of Shelley and Milton against T. S. Eliot's
attacks had been a paradoxical defence of their classicism of style; his influential essay on metre a defence of
using classical terms to describe English poetry[14]; and
his finest work of literary history, awkwardly entitled
(as part of a series) *English Literature in the Sixteenth
Century excluding Drama* (1954), extolled the 'golden'
voice of Sir Philip Sidney and Edmund Spenser, as
opposed to 'drab', in a critical climate in which Metaphysicals like Donne and Herbert counted for more than
their courtly forerunners among the Elizabethans. This
was a classical mind. The introduction to medieval and
Renaissance literature that appeared some months after
his death as *The Discarded Image* (1964), based on the
accumulated notes of lectures he had given for decades
in Oxford and Cambridge, deals sympathetically with
authors who, as he approvingly remarks, quote Homer
and Hesiod 'as if they were no less to be taken into
account than the sacred writers'; and the break in the

European spirit he saw as a consequence of the seven-teenth-century scientific revolution is magnified here, in a sweeping argument, far beyond the familiar classroom shift from the Middle Ages to the Renaissance. It is a shock, no doubt, to find so humanistic a writer denigrating Renaissance humanism, which he saw as philistine and obscurantist: the New Learning, he believed, created the New Ignorance. But this is not an easily predictable intelligence, and he associated humanism with book-burning extremists and a rule-bound notion of literature which would, if England had followed France into a restrictive classicism, have castrated its literature and thwarted the genius of Shakespeare, Milton and Bunyan. He loved what the humanists did in reviving the Ancients, and hated the ferocity of their adversarial style: 'If their manners were often like those of giants, so were their labours'.[15] His rhetorical mastery, in the end, is a mastery of praise, unlike Leavis's, and it flourishes best where a tribal loyalty combines with an issue of faith. The temper of the Book of Common Prayer, he once wrote,

> may seem cold to those reared in other traditions, but no one will deny that it is strong. It offers little, and concedes little, to merely natural feelings: even religious feelings it will not heighten till it has first sobered them; but at its greatest it shines with a white light hardly surpassed outside the pages of the New Testament itself.[16]

★　　★　　★

In the 1960s the British critical tradition split between history and theory. I shall consider only the first of these here, since theory has no independent insular life, and in an order only partly chronological.

Post-war Britain found its own literary history, at least since mid-Victorian times, still unwritten. That left a lot to do. Academic English was a recent invention, largely of the inter-war years; and even where it existed it had commonly stopped with the early nineteenth century. The study of Chaucer, Shakespeare and their contemporaries was not much better off. Before the 1950s there was no such thing as a critical study of *Piers Plowman*, for example, or of *Sir Gawain and the Green Knight*. In these circumstances the critical historian was forced to be original, and literary history was perforce boldly innovative. Kathleen Tillotson's *Novels of the 1840s* (1954) linked the fiction of Dickens, Thackeray, Elizabeth Gaskell and the Brontës to the social history of their times, exploring the techniques of serial publication, and in a concentrated masterpiece of creative scholarship it demonstrated how intimately public events affect literature, and literature in its turn events. Frank Kermode's first book, *Romantic Image* (1957), elegantly demonstrated how the image of Modernist poetry was not discontinuous from late Victorian critical ideas, connecting the poems of Yeats and Eliot to their forebears in the 1890s. In *The Victorian Sage* (1953) John Holloway revived the faded reputations of Carlyle, Disraeli, George Eliot, Newman, Arnold and Hardy as controversialists, and set himself to show, as a trained philosopher, how Wittgensteinian analysis could be brought to bear on their forgotten polemics. These are all writings by academics in early or middle life; and though animated as argument, they are deliberately cast in an academic mould. Donald Davie's *Purity of Diction in English Verse* (1952), by contrast, is touched with the spirit of the manifesto: the first book of young poet and lecturer who, though still a Leavisite, was eager to prepare the way for a critical acceptance of his own verse. The book is an imaginative outgrowth of practical criticism, but it

breaks new ground in its choice of late Augustan poets –
Charles Wesley and Samuel Johnson – and (by a bold
leap of association) Wordsworth, Coleridge and the later
Romantics: its chapter on 'Shelley's urbanity', paradoxical in its very title, showing the entry of a commanding new critical voice. The book registers a new-found
fascination with Ezra Pound, too, on whom Davie was
soon to write two books, as opposed to T. S. Eliot –
espousing a failed Modernist against the acknowledged
leader of London literary opinion – and its tactic of
saying-the-other-thing was soon to become the mark of
a critic eager to clear a space for himself and for others of
like mind. The book might, in its day, have served as a
poetic manifesto for the Movement – a sort of critical
defence of the Angry Young Poet – but events were to
take another turn, leading him in 1968 to settle in the
United States for twenty years; to produce, on his
return, *Under Briggflats* (1989), a critical history of British
poetry since 1960.

All these instances illustrate the radical possibilities of
historical thought. An age defines itself by choosing
another age – usually a forgotten or neglected age – to
teach itself new manners through old customs. History
can make one's own world look different. The Victorians had favoured the medieval, Modernists the seven-
teenth-century Metaphysicals, Bloomsbury and the Sitwells the early eighteenth century. The poets and critics
of the 1950s shifted their gaze towards poets who had
worked after the death of Pope, novelists who followed
Jane Austen, critics of culture who followed William
Cobbett. Such shifts of view are dedicated and tactical
all at once. A self-defining attitude struck by an aspiring
mind can, in an instant, turn into a conviction passionately held. Then it mellows. 'If critics have any
reason for existence,' one of them has said, 'this is it: to
give assurance of value, and to provide somehow –

perhaps anyhow – the means by which readers may be put in possession of the valuable book.'[17] The critical moment was not folly, and it has left monuments which, though now mostly neglected, deserve to last. To abandon the past, and knowledge of the past, is always to abandon more than that. It is to surrender all purposeful hope of changing, through literature or any other means, the world in which one is bound to live.

6

Poets

In British poetry since the war, generations have met, clashed and overlapped.

That is partly an effect of long life. Robert Graves (1895–1985), a resident of Spain from 1929, was born when Victoria was still Queen, and he was writing verse almost down to his death at the age of ninety. A generation of the 1930s, meanwhile – Auden, MacNeice, Day Lewis and Spender – though depleted by emigration, were still at work after 1945; and the finest volume of Dylan Thomas (1914–53), *Deaths and Entrances* (1946), appeared only months after the war ended. Basil Bunting (1900–87), a pre-war disciple of Ezra Pound, was publishing verse in the 1930s but, after a war spent in Iran, achieved fame as a poet only in the 1960s. A still younger generation of poets arrived in the early 1950s, with the new reign. But neo-Elizabethan verse has proved far different from Elizabethan. It is characteristically spare and angular; and compared with the traditions of Eliot and Thomas which it displaced, given to tighter and more traditional metrical forms, and notably more candid and more accessible. 'Hearing one saga, we enact the next', as Donald Davie began one of his most quoted poems, 'Remembering the Thirties', meaning that one generation of poets provokes another. But such provocations are commonly reactive, and each poetic wave seeks to define itself less by imitation than by contrast against the last.

A few elements, it is true, hardly change. The prevailing poetic mode, regardless of generation, is short-breathed and even fragmentary. David Jones's *The Sleeping Lord and Other Fragments* (1974) is content to present itself as a heap of drafts, in prose as well as verse, with occasional footnotes to explain the Welsh; the name-poem itself, composed in 1966–7, being prefaced by a note that calls the whole work fragmentary and the title itself no more than provisional. The sleeping lord is the land of Britain, so that the theme (if nothing else) smacks of the epic; but that purpose, if it was ever there at all, never emerges beyond intention. Brevity predominates everywhere. There are no post-war epics, and the charge of minor – whether in status or in aspiration – has often hung menacingly over the verse of the age. It is certainly a tradition remarkable for the things of major interest it has voluntarily abandoned. It has largely abandoned the lyric since Dylan Thomas died, verse drama since Eliot and Christopher Fry stopped writing for the stage, and epic from the start. If epic means a noble narrative drawn from an heroic past, then it has flourished since 1945 only in prose – in Tolkien's *Lord of the Rings*, perhaps, or Paul Scott's *Raj Quartet* on the end of British India, or Bruce Chatwin's *Songlines* (1987), which deals as a travel-book with mythical Australian aborigines who once sang the earth into being as they walked. Those sound like epic themes. But they are all in prose, and one only has to try to imagine anything as vast in verse to realise how sub-Homeric the post-war poetic tradition has been content to remain.

All that is something to concede at the start. Compared with the dynamic life of fiction and drama, British poetry has been widely seen to be minimal and modest. 'A lot of little people' Philip Larkin once called the modern tradition of verse in a 1973 radio interview, defending his new anthology *The Oxford Book of Twentieth-Century Verse* (1973) after he had spent five years, as an editor, reading it all. That was to speak realistically, and in no way condescendingly. Littleness – the love of the miniature – can after all be an aspiration of poetry, and a boast. Small is beautiful, and not everyone is trying to be a Homer. The new tone, at its most characteristic, is knowingly rueful and commonly born of a professional training in literature, where the poet – an analyst, now, rather than a prophet – is intent on standing well outside his own emotions: so far outside, sometimes, that they have almost ceased to be his. Donald Davie caught something of that mood in his autobiography when he called Cambridge poetry in his time 'sensitive, intelligent, well-mannered, but never conclusively and passionately clinched'[1] – oddly attributing all that to the distinctive light and climate of East Anglia, though his account might as easily sum up the entire post-war poetry of the British Isles. For the larger ambitions of mind and spirit, the poet is often content to imply, one must look to prose.

★   ★   ★

Why is this? One contributory reason may have been the loss of hegemony by native poets in the years between the wars. For the first and (so far) last time, post-war poets born in the British Isles found a literary tradition broken and power held by alien hands. In an age in which nationalism was a natural mode of thought, even in the arts, the loss was felt, resented, and even spasmodically resisted. 'The great enemy,' Robert Graves used to say, 'is this Franco-American thing', meaning Ezra Pound and T. S. Eliot writing in the spirit of Laforgue, or the ageing W. B. Yeats who tried to be influenced by Pound, or the classic age of American poets between the wars with Wallace Stevens, Robert Frost and William Carlos Williams. Wherever such poets may have chosen to live, they had plainly worshipped un-British gods. Eliot may have turned Anglican and taken British citizenship in the late 1920s, but down to the 1940s his politics remained obstinately French *ultra* and wholly outside British affairs; and his role in literary politics, like Pound's, remained by choice that of a French coterie leader. When Yeats died in the south of France in January 1939, he was treated with only distant and qualified admiration by W. H. Auden, in an eloquent elegy written from New York, where he had settled in that very month. No native-born poet after the early death of Dylan Thomas in 1953, at the age of thirty-nine, struck a British note in verse that was widely noticed or loved by the world till John Betjeman's *Collected Poems* of 1958; though Robert Conquest's slim anthology of Movement poets, *New Signatures* (1956), persuaded a few readers that Lucky Jim could write in verse as well as prose. The British poet staged something like a return in the 1950s, beyond a doubt. But if he harboured any respect for the older tradition of Modernism, he failed by that fact alone to fit the new and defiant mood of the times. In 1959 Davie protested about 'a conspiracy to pretend that Eliot and Pound never happened',[2] and emigrated to California nine years later. This was contested territory. The return of the natives, when it happened, like that of Tolkien's little people at the close of *The Lord of the Rings*, was arduous and bitter. They found a ruined landscape, fragments of the idols of alien gods and fields barren of grain.

The ruin had begun before the invasion of Modernists in the 1910s, and there are some evidences of an enemy within. The great difficulty is ultimately one of stuff. What is the stuff of poetry? Literature, when it matters, has something to say, and it matters a lot when it has a lot to say: something urgently new, perhaps, or perhaps

something urgently old, since mankind as often needs
to recall ancient truths as to learn new ones. In the early
twentieth century, unfortunately, poetry had too seldom attempted either. It had abandoned meaning.

That was an oddity of the age. There is nothing
inherently impossible, after all, about the notion of great
intellectual discoveries announced in verse. Dante and
Milton did it; Pope attempted it; Wordsworth's *Prelude*
and, in the opinion of many, Tennyson's *In Memoriam*
had managed it too. Then the line runs thin, and
perhaps Robert Bridges's *Testament of Beauty* (1929) is the
last long poem in England to try to proclaim urgent
truths – some of them heretical – to a troubled time. The
book, which was dedicated to George V, was respectfully reviewed, and it sold. But its ultimate failure, intellectual and artistic, was plain to his successor-poets long
before Auden emigrated to America in 1939. This was
the end of a line, and it leaves only scattered and
small-scale achievements to be considered. Thomas
Hardy, when he died in 1928, left behind a poetic legacy
at once impressive and uncomfortable: uncomfortable
in that it survives only in snatches – short poems by the
hundreds but no pre-eminent masterpiece, and not
even a single isolable collection of generally acknowledged short masterpieces, since everyone's list of Hardy's best poems differs, and understandably differs,
from everyone else's. The problem persists. John Heath-
Stubbs's *Artorius* (1973), for example, a work on King
Arthur which the poet himself has called a heroic poem,
is more like a medley in verse and prose than a single
work, being loosely built around the zodiac, the nine
Muses and the labours of Hercules, including a surprising satire of F. R. Leavis as Phyllidulus delivering a
tedious academic lecture. Heath-Stubbs counts as the
most notable poet of the Christian revival, though he
admired Charles Williams rather than Tolkien and never

knew C. S. Lewis; but the real energy of that revival, it is altogether clear, went into prose. The long poem, since 1945, has look stranded; since it has no readers, it draws few writers. 'I can't be bothered to read long poems,' Norman MacCaig remarked in June 1989, in a radio interview. 'Why should I be bothered to write them?'

★   ★   ★

The poem entered the new reign in 1952 uncertain of its purpose and even of its life. That life revived, but in a manner not evidently continuous, so that the historian feels rather like an explorer in a desert littered, after weary miles, with fragments of uncertain age. But though fragmentary in utterance, the poet can still be vatic in critical aspiration: the conscience of his race, the purifier of its dialect. 'Poetry is responsible,' one of them has said: 'an exemplary exercise, and he [the poet] exists to protest against the debasement of language by which innocence and justice are lost.'[3]

Such are the larger claims that can be made. The difficulty has been to match them with performance, and British poetry has long been haunted by a sense of the unambitious. In his introduction to the Penguin *New Poetry* (1961) A. Alvarez prescribed as instant therapy a new urgency of theme; but the successor-volume of twenty years later – the *Penguin Book of Contemporary British Poetry* edited by Blake Morrison and Andrew Motion – speaks cautiously only of 'a shift of sensibility' since the 1960s, no more; and it derides the easy notion, as they saw it, that poetry excels by its matter. A challenge to show itself as significant had been offered and rejected. Alvarez had deserted verse for prose, notably in *The Savage God* (1971), a study of suicide, as if reconciled by then to the view that in verse, at least, gentility is always bound to win; and a younger poet,

James Fenton, derided his challenge in light-hearted, confident terms:

> He tells you in the sombrest notes
> If poets want to get their oats
> The first step is to slit their throats
> The way to divide
> The sheep of poetry from the goats
> Is suicide.

Fenton's *A German Requiem* (1980), on the other hand, attempts to meet the challenge head-on, since its theme is unashamedly urgent – the destruction of Germany under Hitler and its shocked aftermath:

> It is not what he wants to know.
> It is what he wants not to know.
> It is not what they say
> It is what they do not say.

That is exceptionally daring, as a topic. But far more of the new verse, like the Martian school of Craig Raine, is given to seeing ordinary earthbound reality with the amused or bemused eye of a visitor from another planet, and it illustrates the strictures of those who find British poetry too easily resigned to its own littleness.

> Rain is when the earth is television
> It has the property of making colours darker. . . .

A tradition has descended into ingenuity, prettiness, triviality. It lacks an horizon and looks devoid of urgency and scope.

★   ★   ★

The lack of horizon has its technical aspects. British poetry after 1945 inherited two tempos from the inter-war years, one fast and one slow. The fast, which belonged above all to Yeats, was dynamic and lyrical; and Dylan Thomas sustained it in some of his finest lyrics – 'Poem in October', for example, or 'Fern Hill' – which can only be read at high speed. Thomas, though he achieved only a handful of poems of lasting worth, was a technician who elaborately explored and ex-hausted the range of possibilities of end-rhyme in English, including assonance: stanzaic poems as highly wrought, metrically speaking, as any in the language, but where the effect of metrical honing has been to efface itself, so that they create a delusive sense of ease and sudden release – demanding to be read, rather as childhood is lived, *prestissimo*. His technical erudition, largely obscured in his lifetime by a far-famed bohemian pose, was partly revealed in a broadcast he made in 1946 on Wilfred Owen, when he remarked approvingly that Owen was always 'experimenting technically, deeper and deeper driving towards the final intensity of lan-guage: the words behind words', all poetry being 'in its nature an experiment'.[4] But then the fast lane of poetry, as on motorways, takes only machines of high technical accomplishment.

The slow lane, which was Eliot's, was accomplished in another way: ruminative and gently probing, it de-manded deliberation in reading. Eliot was so great a name in the English-speaking world after 1945, his poems carrying an ultimate promise of intellectual pro-fundity as well as of stylistic accomplishment, that it was difficult for many not to see his example as manda-tory. His was a tradition of verse that was contempla-tive, learned, and profound. It demanded that each phrase, sometimes each word, should be rolled on the tongue like scripture, and Geoffrey Hill echoed its

doctrine when he spoke of the poet protesting against
the debasement of language by modern industrial civilisation, of his bounden duty to purify the speech of his
tribe. In a university-trained atmosphere, this was the
tradition in which almost all young poets, for a time,
were earnestly trained. They grew up wanting to re-
write *Four Quartets*.

That neo-Eliotian tone can sometimes succeed. The
new poetry lacks Eliot's apocalyptic vision, on the
whole, but it can be gently, ruminatively analytical, and
its pace (at least) is often reminiscient of the Master. It
declines to be read at speed:

> You turn and
> hold me tightly, do
> you know who
> I am or am I
> your mother or
> the nearest human being to
> hold on to in a
> dreamed pogrom

as Thom Gunn wrote in 'Touch' (1967), where the
language moves slowly and caressingly, as befits a
love-poem. It is not easy to make verse sound so
unhurried, and the poem escapes its sources, since Eliot
never wrote love-poetry. But then if a dialect is to be
purified, the job of the poet is to make words, regardless
of theme, count as single droplets; and a lyrical storm,
Thomas-style, would destroy that claim. When Dylan
Thomas died in 1953 he was quickly relegated as a
model: this was felt to be a moment to slow down and
catch one's breath. For the oncoming generation of
poets, Eliot and not Yeats was the exemplar, the pace
was deliberate, and each word was held to account.

The outcome of all this was fragmentary, mainly

because the poet – deliberative or not – had no established role to play in an age of prose, and never much of
an assured audience. The problem of finding a public for
verse was never easily solved, but there were broadly
three possibilities, which I shall consider in turn.

The first possibility was *confessional*. On a head-count,
most serious poems in English since 1945, and probably
most British poems too, have been in that mode. Thom
Gunn, who was born in 1929, emigrated to California in
the 1950s after the publication of *Fighting Terms* (1954) –
the youngest poet of the Movement, lost almost as soon
as found – but he has revealingly described in prose
how a poem suddenly arises from a sudden happening
in life which, on reflection, takes on the significance of a
centre of gravity – a sort of collecting-box for wandering
notions of mind, 'an embodiment for my haunting
cluster of concepts', usually unrecognised at the time of
occurrence and seen to cohere only after days or
weeks.[5] The happening, in the case he speaks of, was a
chance encounter with a naked family on a Californian
beach; and yet the resultant poem, as he perceives,
might have been triggered by almost anything, its
source by then largely indecipherable even when it is
remembered and declared. Nor are his poems, though
often broadly confessional, highly revealing of the tortured being of the poet himself. Naked is the best
disguise, and confessionals can be paradoxically private:
a mask to character, as priestly confessions sometimes
are, it is said, rather than an act of candour and
self-avowal.

That reticence is perhaps more British than American.
American poetry since Walt Whitman's 'Song of Myself'
(1855) has been overwhelmingly confessional in its
claims, and never more so than in post-war years,
notably with Robert Lowell and Sylvia Plath; so that it is

natural here to see British poets as hesitant followers in a tradition essentially transatlantic. To that extent the models for this mode of verse are bound to be American, even if some models are shunned rather than embraced. The British tradition is simply not bold enough to supply adequate precedents here. Wordsworth and Tennyson were not confessional in that sense: *The Prelude* and *In Memoriam*, though autobiographical, evolve strategies, much as the British in conversation do to this day, to maintain for their authors a place secure from public gaze. Untouched, on the whole, by traditions of Freudian self-revelation, such confessions stop well short of embarrassment, and there is in any case a national reluctance to self-dramatise. Donald Davie remarks in *These the Companions* (1982) that his heart goes out to poets like Hardy and Eliot who are 'devoted to past styles as to a way of saying and yet not saying, laying bare and yet covering up, confessional and reticent at once.' That sounds duly cautious. Douglas Dunn, a Scottish poet whose *Elegies* (1985) lovingly commemorate the death of a wife, even contrives to maintain the decorum of married life in poems that strikingly record the outward incidents of happy union and tragic bereavement:

> My love had lusty eagerness and style.
> Propriety she had, preferring grace
> Because she saw more virtue in its wit . . .
> Then hear her in her best sardonic style:
> 'Write out of me, not out of what you read',

he wrote in 'Tursac'. These are poems about a private grief that blend passion with a careful decorum, and the poet has declined to read them in public for fear of cheapening a remembered happiness and the loss they delicately record.

Ted Hughes, similarly, who succeeded John Betjeman

as poet laureate on his death in 1984, has kept a
courageous silence on the suicide of his first wife Sylvia
Plath, and his poems work through metaphors of beasts
and birds of prey rather than self-revelation – a sort of
displaced violence where personal tragedy is viewed, if
at all, only through parallels and analogues. This is a
studiously moderate tradition. The enormous international poetic fashion, America-led, for no-holds-barred
confessionals that followed Robert Lowell's *Life Studies*
in 1959 has left some mark on it; but the inherent
indecency of the mode left it looking alien and ultimately cheapening, and Eliot's famous remark in 'Tradition
and the Individual Talent' (1919) about the poet's
'escape from personality' has continued to convince. In
the insular view, at least, emotions so easily released are
unlikely to be authentic, profound, or even interesting.
To spill out is not to confess a valued secret, but to
declare how little it is to be valued.

The second attitude, more rewarding, has been the
mask or *eccentric stance*.
A mask is an invented personality, like Betjeman's or
Larkin's, though often partly real. This is beyond doubt
the richest vein of all; and its roots, like the roots of
modern fiction, are largely eighteenth-century, in Pope
and Cowper. As a tradition it flowered mightily in
Byron, above all in the last cantos of *Don Juan*; trickled
down through some lesser nineteenth-century lights
like Arthur Hugh Clough and W. S. Gilbert, and so to
W. H. Auden in the 1930s – the great Byronist of the
century who wrote a verse 'Letter to Lord Byron' for
Letters from Iceland (1937) and, after the war, a notable
critical essay on *Don Juan*. Auden was followed in short
order by the young John Betjeman, but the whole
tradition that leads to Philip Larkin and beyond is easier
to name than to characterise, easier to illustrate than to

define. It has few equivalents in other lands, even
English-speaking lands. It arises out of a highly insular
tradition of conversation: amusingly semi-learned talk,
richly allusive, vivified by a speaker into social performance – the British, as foreigners often remark, tending to
be actors, or at least mimics – and by a speaker conscious of himself as a character and eager to impart that
consciousness to others, whether as entertainment, self-
defensive deceit, or both; the whole, if you are a poet,
being cast into verse, most characteristically rhyming
verse, to sharpen the sense of performance. Its subject-
matter has to do with the world under the noses of its
readers, or at their daily ears, much as realistic fiction
does – Betjeman was the first poet of the English suburb
– but it is marked, as fiction less consistently is, by a
sustained flippancy of mood that can sometimes veil a
deep and tortured commitment of purpose. That purpose can be tragic, however flippant the manner, and it
can embrace compassion, hatred and dread.

The eccentric stance, then, represents a revived presence of comic realism in that most unlikely of places,
the short poem. The English poet has survived, and in
an age he would be the first to call unpoetic, by
behaving in a manner most of his readers would also
call unpoetic: by mimicking the voices and personalities
of others, by mocking familiar social custom, by parody-
ing past masters and exploiting the absurdity of bardic
pretensions – his own and others – in an essentially
suburban age. Since comic realism has long since trium-
phed in drama and fiction, why not in verse? It was a
thought that was bound to occur to somebody.

The stance, there in Auden in the 1930s and in Eliot's
Old Possum's Book of Practical Cats (1939), was after all in
working order before 1945. Larkin's last published
poem, 'Aubade',[6] is a taxing instance. It is about the fear
of death, which is nothing like a comic subject; but the

very title is faintly comic, since it teasingly suggests an amorous song at dawn, whereas this dawn finds the poet alone and terrified:

> Waking at four to soundless dark, I stare.
> In time the curtain-edges will grow light.
> Till then I see what's really always there:
> Unresting death . . .

and he lies in unheroic pose contemplating a catastrophe which, in its very nature, has no solution:

Being brave
Lets no one off the grave.

It would be stretching terms outrageously to call this a comic poem, and it may be asked why a view so likely to be sincere should be called a pose at all. It purposes to terrify the reader, after all, and probably succeeds. But the pertly dismissive manner of its opening – 'I work all day and get half drunk at night' – startles the poet himself into a grim chuckle that takes him outside the horror of his own mind and leaves him looking back at it; and the smart phrase about religion – that 'vast moth-eaten musical brocade/Created to pretend we never die' – achieves a satirical concision which, though it may not console, effectively leaves the poet looking wry in his anxiety. To see oneself as clearly as this is to see oneself as someone else.

Jokes, in this tradition, need not trivialise; and the essence of the eccentric stance, which draws attention to the poet's own oddity as well as the world's, is that it can be tragic as well as comic, or (better still) tragic and comic at the same time. The tradition of Byron, Auden and Betjeman that Larkin inherited in the 1950s is like good talk put to rhyming verse, since full-bodied rhyme (as Byron and W. S. Gilbert knew) gives bite to a joke; and calling religion a moth-eaten musical brocade sounds like the sort of remark a clever man might make when half-drunk among friends. Larkin mined that vein hard in his later verse, at least from the second of his four lifetime collections, *The Less Deceived* (1955), after a youth misspent (as he came to see) in trying to write like Yeats; and his posthumous *Collected Poems* (1988), issued three years after his death, shows how long and uncertain the road was. It has an adolescent appendix that starts in 1938, when he was sixteen, followed by an early manhood in which he tried to write first like Yeats and then like Hardy, whose poems in 1966 he provocatively called 'many times over the best body of poetic work this century has so far to show'.[7] That must be a smack at Yeats, Pound and Eliot, all three; and it may imply that Hardy's greatness lay unregarded partly because he was a native in an age when to be thought a great poet was to be born out of England; partly because his collected poems, though totalling over eight hundred pages, seldom include anything more than two pages long. Hardy's was a high achievement of scattered occasions, and as such it seems obstinately to resist the title of greatness. But Larkin's late accolade suggests too that Eliot's *Four Quartets*, as fragmentary in their construction as *The Waste Land* had been, left no working models to his successors for writing verse *in extenso*. In the late twentieth century the poem is classically, almost necessarily, short.

Brevity raises problems of its own, whether for masters of eccentricity or for social realists. Realism is traditionally a mode that has felt free to make a lot of space for itself, and in the eighteenth century Samuel Richardson could take a million words or so to make a point about the sexual morality of the age. The realist-poet, by contrast, has more recently worked like a cat-burglar: he finds an easy entrance, moves fast once he is inside, grabs only what looks small and precious, and is out of the place in a minute or two. All that has the considerable advantage of demanding of a writer no significant investment of time: a short poem can be written between sitting down and standing up. It would not have suited Richardson, as a way of work. But cat-burgling was always Larkin's way; and it was mainly Betjeman's, too, before him, from *Mount Zion* (1932) down to *A Few Late Chrysanthemums* (1954) and *A Nip in the Air* (1974). Only in his long verse-autobiography *Summoned by Bells* (1960) did Betjeman abandon poetic brevity, for the first and last time, but he paid the price of abandoning stylistic concision too, and the work is little more than a series of incidents strung out, neck-lace-like, along a remembered life. It is not seriously a continuum, and it leaves the problem of the long poem looking as insoluble as ever.

There have been numberless attempts, none the less, to solve it. Vikram Seth, an Indian schooled in England, has essayed the verse novel in *The Golden Gate* (1984), a satire of San Francisco life more Byronic than anything else. But that is a sport, and Auden's preference for the short poem was to be Betjeman's and ultimately Larkin's: a form radically uspacious and dedicated, on the whole, to a single point. The post-war poem tends to be a swollen epigram, sometimes simply an epigram. There is a three-line poem by Gavin Ewart, for example, called 'Existences' (*The Collected Ewart*, Random Century, 1960), that makes the simple point that whoever and wherever you are you cannot win:

Living at Potato Point and dying of Dog's Disease.

Living in The Blue Desert, and dying of inertia.

Alive in Quick City, and fading with the trendsetters.

That is paring all the way down to the bone; and some others, collected in Ewart's *All My Little Ones* (1978), are no more than one-liners. No doubt the total economy of a poet's life encourages brevity. Poetry is an under-paid profession, unlike the novelist's, and poets' publishers do not usually pay advances. On the other hand, it is a question whether the post-war poet would know how to keep an argument going, Milton-fashion, over thousands of lines at a stretch, or want to know. Brevity is his need as well as his choice, and he is happy with it.

The thread of eccentricity in English verse is varied but unbroken. Betjeman and Larkin were friends. Larkin met Auden only once, and later professed that though he admired his early poems he could see little virtue in anything he wrote after settling in the United States in 1939.[8] If these are the three great eccentrics of twentieth-century verse – the Byronists of the new age – then they can most briskly be distinguished in terms of social rank: Auden of Anglo-Catholic professional background, scion of the sort of bookish family that utters scraps of curious learning at mealtime and solves the hardest of crossword puzzles, to the consternation of guests, at breakfast; Betjamin of businessman father and belonging to a manufacturing world he refused to enter, so that his snobbery is internal to the British middle classes and full of the superiority of one bourgeois suburb over another, as Hampstead is superior to Golders Green or old wealth to new. (Aristocracy and the lower orders hardly come into it, except as figures in a landscape.) That is an instructive emphasis. People sometimes need to be reminded, or told, that a one-class world can be a snobbish one, and that to achieve a one-class society would not be to achieve an equal one; and Betjeman's poetry makes that useful point – worrying angrily, affectionately, compassionately, contemptuously about how other people can be what they are, dress as they choose, live as they do. Most citizens of an industrial or post-industrial land inhabit a suburb, after all, trying to better themselves and noticing how their neighbours do it, or fail to do it, and it was Betjeman's arresting achievement to bring the suburb – that neglected theme that is always likely to resist epic or lyric handling and yield itself up all too easily to satire – into the range of poetic art.

Larkin's poems, by contrast, are not primarily about other people at all. His parentage, which was respectable, counts for little here. The poems record an inner voice, with its haunting disquiets and abject accommodations to outer experience. It was a reading of Hardy's poems, he tells, that first taught him to dare to listen to himself and trust what he heard when he did, 'not to be afraid of the obvious'; which is perhaps why he thought of himself as a romantic, since listening to oneself is what romantics are supposed to do. The dictum of Hardy he most loved to quote was 'The poet takes note of nothing that he cannot feel'. But Larkin seldom writes just like Hardy even if, in his last two collections – *The Whitsun Weddings* (1964) and *High Windows* (1974) – one everywhere senses a debt. That debt is partly negative. Like Hardy, he avoids the pomp of language in favour of the blunt and the penetrating; he eschews the mandarin and stabs hard at the point without circumlocution or fuss. And in the cat-burglar school of verse one point is easily enough, even for the best poem.

Larkin's sense of society, however, was at least as strong as Hardy's, in its own way, which is why his poems survive in their modest corpus less as romance than as social realism. His singular triumph, in the end, was to write social realism about himself. That is a paradox that needs to be probed. First, he turned himself into a character, much as Betjeman and Auden had done, though a modest temperament never allowed him to follow Betjeman into the worldly successes of a media man. Then he analysed the character he had partly inherited and partly created, which was the being he had in truth become; whereas Betjeman is seldom self-analytical, at least for long, and generalises outward rather than testing a sentiment or a mood. That, oddly enough, leads Larkin not towards introspection but into miniature portraits of British life. In a 1961 poem called 'Breadfruit', for example, which he never collected – perhaps because he thought it too flippant – he summarises a social world which, as a life-long bachelor, he had long observed and never lived. The poem helps to explain why he never lived it. It is a social summary, executed in high colloquial concision and an unblinking accuracy that reminds the reader of his friend Kingsley Amis, and it quickly turns itself into a sort of Amis novel-in-little:

> A mortgaged semi- with a silver birch;
> Nippers; the widowed mum; having to scheme
> With money; illness; age. So absolute
> Maturity falls, when old men sit and dream
> Of naked native girls who bring breadfruit
>   Whatever they are.[9]

An affected ignorance about breadfruit is part of the assumed comic tone here – an adopted pose. Larkin as a university librarian only had to look them up to find out; but 'absolute maturity' is a memorably telling euphemism for senility, a tragic point broken across two lines and lightly buried beneath a comic surface to lighten its force. The poem, though amusingly social in content, is somehow ultimately self-exploring, and the watcher forever remains the strongest presence in the work. This, one concludes, is how Larkin saw his world, and nobody else; this is why he lived as he did.

The eccentric mode follows a path, then, that can be lightly traced. With Auden the poet looked at the Western world; with Betjeman at England, or at one large part of it, a suburban middle class; and with Larkin at Larkin. 'Breadfruit' is not just about the familiar social pattern of desire, procreation and dying; it is still more about the mind that sees it, ponders it, and grimly accepts it, at least as a spectacle. Betjeman, unlike Larkin, was at once a devout man and a snob – a suburban who hated most suburbs, though not his own – and he would have rejected the semi-detached house with a silver birch as vulgar and lacking in spiritual substance. Larkin, a wholly secular being, thinks life in any case pointless; but then if pointlessness is all there is, one can be amused and instructed by a lack of point. He is a poet sometimes hopeless but never indignant, and that in an age given to easy indignation, real and assumed. Life is to be borne, he implies, not protested about, as Auden and Betjeman had protested. Wordsworth's wise passiveness here turns rueful and acquiescent: life is what you put up with. By almost complaining, Larkin taught his age how not to complain: much as in 'Church Going' (1954), the poem that made him famous in his early thirties, he showed how by almost worshipping one need not worship. When he died in December 1985, in the same week as two much older poets, Robert Graves and Geoffrey Grigson, he had recorded for a Britain already affluent a world that had passed away: a world of thrift and rationing, of narrow horizons and thwarted hopes. 'Deprivation to me', he once remarked, 'is what daffodils were to Wordsworth.' It was natural for the world at large to imagine that, as a poet of the 1960s and after, he was busy depicting life around him. In fact he was a poet of recorded time, like Wordsworth: the survivor, remembrancer and interpreter of a dour age gone dead and threatened with oblivion.

The third mode of post-war poetry – the smallest, probably, in bulk, but perhaps the most distinguished in achievement – has been the assertion of high and ancient *commonplace*.

That is the classic mode of European poetry since ancient times, and the intimidating strength of great anthology-poems out of past centuries: remembered single lines out of Shakespeare, or Gray's Elegy – 'The paths of glory lead but to the grave' – or Keats. Everyone knows about it. Every poet, one imagines, would like to pull it off, at least once in a lifetime. Even Modernists like Eliot and post-Modernists like Dylan Thomas, notorious as they are for their difficulty and seemingly proud of it, occasionally let a line escape out of convolution into a clarity Lucretius or Dante might have envied. Eliot achieved it when he wrote 'Death by Water', the shortest and plainest section of *The Waste Land*, which ends 'Remember Phlebas, who was once handsome and tall as you'. Thomas, even more incongruously, in 'A Refusal to Mourn the Death, by Fire, of a Child in London' in *Deaths and Entrances* (1946), emerges triumphantly, and only after infinite syntactical intricacy, into a final lapidary line: 'After the first death, there is no other' – a line only seemingly simple, in this instance, since it bears alternative meanings. It is there again in an early poem of Kingsley Amis called 'Masters' from *A Case of Samples* (1956), which concerns the ancient commonplace that one must appear confident in order to be so:

> That horse whose rider fears to jump will fall,
> Riflemen miss if orders sound unsure . . .

the poem begins, and it continues in similar quasi-

proverbial vein, mainly end-stopped, playing quick
variations on a single classic theme. Geoffrey Hill, too,
though he cultivates at times a language as dense as
G. M. Hopkins's, can momentarily achieve classicism of
that sort: many poems in *For the Unfallen* (1959), *King Log*
(1968) and *Tenebrae* (1978) being grimly to do with issues
as bitter as the Crucifixion or Nazism.

> Undesirable you may have been, untouchable
> you were not.

he opens 'September song', telling of a ten-year-old boy
deported during the war to die; and the poem ends with
his own quiet September reflection:

> This is plenty. This is more than enough.

These are all clarities that emerge from contexts that are
radically something else, so that complexity is never left
far behind. In fact they need such contexts to exist and
count at all, and their concentration is an effect of
surrounding mass and circumambient pressures, like
the matter at the heart of the sun.

The commonplace mode, then, though an occasional
inheritance from Moderns as well as Ancients, is the
rarest of triumphs in post-war verse.

It is rare, and improbable, if only because this is a
poetic tradition too firmly tied to the severely occasional
to venture far, or often, into universal assertions. Thom
Gunn has remarked that 'the occasion . . . is the starting
point, only, of a poem', but it is still one 'to which the
poet must in some sense stay true'.[10] Staying true to
your starting-point, whether a sudden intuition about
the human condition, a child killed in a racial pogrom,
or the sudden glimpse of a naked family on a Californian beach, has tended to keep poems not just short in

scale but argumentatively tied, so to speak, by a short string: short in content as well as in length. The situation has advantages and disadvantages all at once. Peter Porter, for example, an Australian-born poet living in London, has collected eight volumes of his verse, beginning with *Once Bitten, Twice Bitten* (1961), into a single volume of *Poems* (1983); and as a learned poet, his starting-points are most commonly sudden encounters with music, painting or literature. In fact his 1983 collection ends with some versions of Martial, most concise of the Roman poets. Poetry of that sort, much of it first written for weekly journals, demands to be brief, since a poem in that tradition needs to be seen at a glance and entire. In fact the reader unconsciously rations his mind to it before he runs his eye through; and if it happens to overlap a page, he may easily find himself turning the page first to establish its total length in his mind before he starts to read at all, as if its brevity were its essence – which it is.

If all experience is suitable to poetry, as Thom Gunn has remarked, 'including Golders Green and acne',[11] then the post-war poet has preferred to see it in atoms: the sudden thought, the passing glimpse, the hint gathered from looking at a sculpture or reading an old book. Even in his longest poem, *Summoned by Bells*, which is mainly in blank verse, Betjeman excuses himself in his preface on the grounds that to have written it in prose would have made it longer. Blank verse may get as near to prose as verse ever can, but verse (he argues) is by its nature short, and prose would have stretched it.

Brevity has been the soul of poetry since Robert Bridges died. It is also its defence, and it needs that defence to live by. Novels can be a seemingly endless riot of words; plays, though usually shorter, take a whole evening, and you have to get to the theatre and get back. A poem, in recent tradition, is at the polar extreme to all that. In Gunn or Porter or Seamus Heaney, in Ted Hughes or Geoffrey Hill, it can most commonly be read in a minute, and two minutes can look like an exceptional investment in the rush of life. No century previous to this has trafficked with poetry exclusively in this way. Such encounters are provisional, uncommitted, and customarily harmless. And perhaps a lack of harm is the last, abiding sense one has of poetry in the post-war age. Dylan Thomas's unforgettable elegy on a dead child, after all, is called a refusal to mourn, even if the title is long and riddling and not to be taken at its word. These are visions of the world that are content to be savoured rather than treasured, and it is not altogether clear that they were meant to last. Betjeman's indignation about suburban vulgarity, always artfully mixed with acceptance – what can you expect of people nowadays? – has died with him, so that he survives in the memory as much a character as a maker of rhymes. Larkin's tragic acceptance of modern life survives as a kind of acceptance – another character – but hardly as tragedy: it is all too rueful and amusing for that. So is Ted Hughes's fascination with beasts and birds of prey, which looks like a violence imported into poetry rather than a mood native to the poet's mind: convincingly part of the experience neither of the creator nor of the reader. A consciously modest world like this, content to see life as fragments rather than to pattern them, like great poets of the past, into meanings, raises the awkward question whether it has achieved much, over half a century, beyond a telling and trivial elegance. Unpretentious it has often been; but then it is a moral rather than an artistic virtue to be that. All great art has pretensions.

It is still, let it be said, a tradition in working order. If the poetic spirit is to do more than survive, it will not be enough, in itself, to speak urgent truths to a troubled time. But some urgency of purpose is what it will need if poetry is to do more than maintain a tradition of verse-making and deliver it intact to another age.

7

Osborne, Pinter, Stoppard

The story of London theatre, by common consent, divides at 1956, when John Osborne's *Look Back in Anger* opened at the Royal Court Theatre.

May 1956 was a moment of change, even revolutionary change; and like many revolutions, it was also a reaction. Before it, a more formal theoretical tradition had tried to restore an Elizabethan sense of poetry to audiences hungry for colour and style. The post-war verse plays of T. S. Eliot and Christopher Fry were born of austerity: in Eliot's case they were an attempt, partly successful, to reach audiences larger than his poetry was ever likely to enjoy; in Fry's, to remind a public battered by war and its aftermath that there is life and joy in the ceremonies of language, at least, if not in daily life itself. The mood was nostalgic, and verse marked a return in many senses. It was a return to the roots of English drama, in Shakespeare; to the roots of English social tradition, too, since it proclaimed the permanence in national life of dignity, ceremony and rank. There was little enough of any of those ancient virtues in Attlee's Britain, but they flourished briefly in London theatre, like exotic plants in a conservatory, with Eliot's *Cocktail Party* (1949) and Fry's *Venus Observed* (1950). Along with bitter-sweet plays by such survivors of pre-war theatre as Noël Coward and Terence Rattigan, they answered to a desperate hope that, in spite of appearances, nothing essential had changed.

The trouble was that something had. It was not, on the whole, a change wrought by politicians, and extensions to a welfare state founded as long ago as 1908 have little to do with the matter. Change is natural to human society, and Britain by the 1950s was new in ways that novelists and dramatists, among others, found puzzling to account for. The war had not abolished social differences, merely entered some new players and shifted some of the rules of the game. Britain was not egalitarian, and it was already clear that it did not seriously want to be. If the young were openly impatient with the old, it was an impatience the old understandably found unspecific, nebulous and ultimately enigmatic. There was a stir in the air, but it was hard to say who was stirring, or why. Osborne's *Look Back* recorded that mixed mood of puzzlement, alarm and hope. Something was afoot, no doubt of it, and audiences were suddenly in a mind less for assurances than for explanations.

The revival of realism in British theatre was slightly, but only slightly, belated. *Look Back* follows the first published novels of Kingsley Amis and Iris Murdoch by only two or three years, and it may have owed less to them than to the groping intuition of a young actor – Osborne was twenty-seven at the time – who had sniffed a mood in the air rather than from the pages of books. Where Eliot and Fry had written about unchanging human verities, Osborne strove to chronicle the urgent moment, and events conspired to help. May 1956, midway in Sir Anthony Eden's short premiership, was not a critical month at home or abroad; but five months later, in October, there were the twin crises of Suez and Hungary, and the reckless young dramatist had proved himself an efficient prophet of doom. The Osborne revolution in British theatre was remarkably swift and apparently effortless, in the event, and in retrospect it is hard to see how it could have failed.

The theatre that welcomed it was and is ample in its provision. It includes nearly fifty commercial theatres in London, along with state-subsidised theatres eventually numbering five – three in the National Theatre that opened in its permanent home on the South Bank in 1976, and two belonging to the Royal Shakespeare Company; and, in addition, a shifting host of fringe theatres, some of them in improbable makeshift surroundings. As a concentration of legitimate theatre, then, London may be more or less unique: between fifty and a hundred performances within two miles of Piccadilly Circus on any weekday of the year, since there is no Sunday theatre except in private clubs; and unlike Paris, they stay open in summer. The proportion devoted to new drama, however, is hard to estimate. Some theatres, it is certain, will be playing revivals; others musicals; others, especially at Christmas, pantomimes. And not all new plays are British. None the less, the choice of new and native plays is wide, though subject to unaccountable periods of lassitude when even respectable dramatists deliver nothing but translations of foreign plays or adaptations of well-known novels, and there is probably nothing like it in the world, at least for a world language.

That, in itself, is a reversal. In the years that followed the peace of 1945, Paris and New York surpassed London in theatrical excitement, and the centre of gravity did not decisively shift till the mid 1950s. Since then Broadway has struggled against high and ever higher production costs, and Paris has been struck by a subtler malaise known as NED or Not Enough Dramatists. The rivals, for whatever reason, have fallen back, and since the 1960s the British have had it mostly their own way in the theatres of the West. The English dramatist, backed by the bravura of the English actor, has been the playman of the Western world: for theatre there is nothing like London.

Beneath the creative tip of that glittering theatrical iceberg lies an enormous and invisible base of the untried and unperformed. About a thousand play-scripts a year, for example, are reported to reach the Royal Court Theatre, where *Look Back* opened in May 1956, or several on any average working day; not one per cent of them, it is reasonable to suppose, being performed at the Court or anywhere else. On the other hand the Court has over thirty playwrights under commission, and is said to accept perhaps one uncommissioned play a year. Outside live theatre, what is more, the scale of creativity is a marvel. BBC television, for example, broadcasts some four hundred plays a year: some newly commissioned, others adapted from plays and novels already in print; and it is reported to receive some eight thousand unsolicited play-scripts every year, of which it accepts perhaps two or three.[1] The survival rate, then, is rather like that of some highly endangered species in a murderous environment, and the modern dramatist works at high risk; or would do so, were it not that he contrives to survive on grants, odd jobs and loans. But however one interprets the figures, one is left dazzled at the thought of so much creative effort, and the sound of all those clacking typewriters is enough to frighten the birds.

★   ★   ★

What sort of being is the new London dramatist?

He is not, or not usually, a man of letters in any traditional sense of the term. Shaw, Pinero, Galsworthy and Somerset Maugham were men of letters; the post-war dramatist, on the other hand, has more often been a man of the theatre and little else, and his training is most characteristically an actor's. Osborne and Pinter both trod the boards before they wrote plays; so did Alan Ayckbourn (b.1939), an actor and stage-manager in repertory theatre, and a BBC radio drama producer (1964–70), before he settled in Scarborough as a prolific writer of comedies and artistic director of the Stephen Joseph Theatre-in-the-Round. Tom Stoppard, exceptionally, was a journalist; and Simon Gray – a plainer counter-instance – an academic: a profession that admittedly finds its uses for the histrionic, however, and he enjoyed a theatrical time as a Cambridge undergraduate before settling in London to lecture. There are odder routes to fame than these. Joe Orton trained as an actor and learned to write plays by typing out a friend's and realising he could do it better: to be murdered by his room-mate in 1967, out of jealousy, at the age of thirty-four. Christopher Marlowe too came to a violent end when young, killed before he was thirty; and it is tempting to call Orton the Marlowe of the British dramatic revival, were it not that he wrote farces and never a tragedy. And there are other dramatists like Caryl Churchill and Timberlake Wertenbaker who emerged out of student theatricals and seem to have a flow of actor-ready language in their veins.

The flourishing of theatre since the 1950s has been firmly based on a familiarity with theatre itself, then, rather than on the printed word. All this was unpredictable in 1956; it was genuinely surprising. In the exhausted atmosphere of post-war London theatre, few if any would have foreseen that London would shortly make of itself the theatrical capital of the Western world; fewer still that an actor could write a better play than a writer. But it is the actor, whether professional or amateur, who in the event has conquered. As Shakespeare and Ben Jonson in the 1590s replaced the University Wits, who were bookish men, so a new breed of performers suddenly replaced the literary world of

Shaw, Priestley and Eliot. They may sometimes need to be taught to spell, but they do not need to be taught theatre: they have ~~known it,~~ one feels, as long as they have known anything. Though they may occasionally preach from their stages, they are not, like Shaw or Eliot, primarily there to edify and convert, and their ultimate loyalty is not to dogma but to theatricality itself. They know the ropes, and do not need to be reminded of Harley Granville-Barker's celebrated dictum that drama is an art, but theatre is an industry. They are part of the industry. Many of them started in it at the bottom, and like strolling players anywhere they are by nature adaptable. One of them, Harold Pinter, may be the supreme instance on earth of a dramatic factotum: he can act, direct and write, whether for live theatre, cinema or television; while Stoppard's comedies are theatrical *tours-de-force* based on a technical originality he has learned from watching, it must be supposed, and from reading. Shakespeare and Jonson began as actors, too, and the parallel with another Elizabethan golden age is richly tempting. These are playwrights who, whatever their training, write speeches that actors can speak, not sermons for moralists to spout. As Shakespeare himself would have said, they are sharp and sententious.

To have worked in theatre, sometimes as a menial, is to take a briskly professional view of what theatre can and cannot do. That, to be sure, is not the only possible view, and an Alternative Theatre still survives as a link with an older man-of-letters concept of what plays are for. Nothing, usually, is more antique than an avant-garde, and it is in Alternative Theatre since the 1960s that ancient values have been mainly cherished: Victorian social criticism, a Shavian view of the playwright as a moralist and a preacher, and a sense of theatrical contrivance that Noël Coward in his younger days would have thought old-fashioned. Intellectuals are backward-looking, by temperament; and to be experimental, in that world, can easily mean imitating the theatrical techniques of the Weimar Republic or critical theories fashionable in Paris a generation and more ago. Commercial theatre, by contrast, tends to be experimental and unconventional. As Bertolt Brecht once pertinently remarked, capitalism is naturally radical, and the money-making theatres of Shaftesbury Avenue are in practice more innovative, both in technique and in ideas, than semi-amateur happenings in half-converted pubs in Islington or Notting Hill. In fact the assumption that commercial theatre, realistic or other, is intellectually or politically cosy could only survive in wilful ignorance of what it habitually does. There is nothing inherently conservative, in any case, about realism, since it is by picturing a real world, as Osborne did, that the playwright seeks to change it; and commercial theatre, in any case, is only sometimes realistic. What sells in West End theatre is no one thing but a swift succession of different things, and the huge success of musicals like Andrew Lloyd Webber's *Cats* (1981), a work daringly based on T. S. Eliot's *Old Possum's Book of Practical Cats*, is hard to reconcile with the view that in London it is only drawing-room comedies with French windows that the wider public will buy or that promoters will back.

Such innovation is intellectual as well as technical. In fact the intellectual innovation of much commercial theatre since 1956 might have been designed to illustrate Brecht's truth that capitalism is naturally radical in its social effects: that the profit-motive is more likely to transform a society, and faster, than the urge to preach at it or to regulate it. It is the avant-garde that has proved itself politically old-hat, trapped as it is in the clichés of Victorian socialism, and playgoers have understandably tired of plays with titles like *Maydays* or *Not Quite Jerusalem* that deal, more in sorrow than in anger, with the predictable failures of the Old Left and the New. That failure, as they know, is largely unsurprising, and they are sophisticated enough not to wish to be told once again that women are often as good as men or that South African apartheid is wicked. Twenty years after his success with *Look Back* at the Royal Court, John Osborne publicly complained that the atmosphere of the theatre, when he re-enters it, depresses him with the fug of old left-wingery and battles long ago. An audience naturally seeks to be stirred and amused, and it will only fitfully tolerate the assumption that theatregoing is a moral duty.

Realism, in some qualified sense – and realism is always qualified – lies at the heart of much, though never all, of London legitimate theatre since 1956, whether kitchen-sink realism or not. The new drama was above all a social drama; and like most things characteristically British in the arts, strongest in the field of the comic. Even its tragedies have tended to be funny. That is not an original paradox, if a paradox at all. *Hamlet*, after all, is a comic play, among other things, and its language sparkles with fun; even the *Oresteia* of Aeschylus, that foundation-stone of European tragedy, has its amusing moments; and only a year before Osborne's *Look Back*, Samuel Beckett's *Waiting for Godot* had opened in London at the Arts Theatre. It was directed by Peter Hall, some twenty years later the first director of the National Theatre, and it is a sparkling tragedy where the cause of the helpless and the hopeless never looked more amusing, written in two languages as if to show that the paradox of the tragi-comic is not exclusively English and that the Irish have always known about it. One may indeed joke about despair; in fact it may be quite the best thing to do about it.

★   ★   ★

Realism, if the word implies a touch of squalor, was a conscious and deliberate choice of the new dramatists, and their immediate predecessors had not in that sense been realists. The ten years of London theatre that followed 1945 had been years of multiple revivalism, but not of squalor. There had been Chekovian plays set in comfortable sitting-rooms, French windows and all, where gentlefolk bemoaned the rigours of austerity in a tone quietly (and rightly) confident that good times would come again. The poetic dramas of T. S. Eliot and Christopher Fry, again, where poetic prose, from the spectator's point of view, merged imperceptibly into dramatic verse, were faintly allusive of the world about them, but more concerned with eternal moral verities than the state of England. Only an abiding emphasis on the comic, though it grows thin at times, is a continuum in this tradition. Eliot's *Cocktail Party*, which opened at the Edinburgh Festival in August 1949, was teasingly subtitled 'a comedy'; its successor, *The Confidential Clerk*, which opened there four years later, was more cautiously subtitled 'a play'; and both were imbued with a spirit of devout resignation, only faintly whimsical, at the spectacle of a fading culture and a world almost too bad to be borne. Fry's plays are less extreme in their assumptions, and more playful. *A Phoenix Too Frequent* (1946), for example, based on an ancient myth, dealt gaily with the classic infidelity of womankind; *The Lady's Not for Burning* (1949) and *Venus Observed* (1950) startled audiences with their sustained verbal prettiness in an age starved by war and rationing for verve and style.

That rococo mood did not last, and by the late 1950s it had been sternly abolished by a younger breed of playwright concerned, as they claimed, not with nostalgia but with the here-and-now. In a boom world like the post-war years, Now can turn into Then rather quickly, and it must be admitted that the kitchen-sink school was touched by a spirit of nostalgia from the start. The hero

of *Look Back* worships the memory of a father who died
of wounds received in the Spanish Civil War; his
father-in-law, a dignified relic of British India, is shown
as amiable and worthy, according to his lights. Base-
ment or attic poverty was after all a vanishing phenomenon when Osborne and Pinter flattered London
audiences in the late 1950s with images of life by the
ironing board or the kitchen sink. But the reaction of
ageing opinion was gratifyingly sharp. 'The health I
have,' wrote a retired Eton schoolmaster, praising the
adrenalin-flow that only hostility can give, 'is largely
due to Leavis and Amis and Osborne and the *New
Statesman*, and the umpire who gave me out in a critical
school-match at Eton.'[2] Hating can be fun, and the new
theatrical realism throve on it. It can also lead to sudden
panic. Noël Coward and Terence Rattigan, both dough-
ty survivors of the witty chandelier-style comedies of
the 1930s, fled London in despair as far as Jamaica or
Hollywood, outraged by what they had seen across the
footlights of West End theatres: dirty kitchens and
ironing boards, draughty attics and a bucket in the
middle of the room to catch the leak. All that put paid,
too, and with dramatic suddenness, to the poetic revival
of Eliot and Fry, which had evidently belonged to a
mood too delicate and tangential to last. It was as if
literature and life had suddenly and startlingly joined
hands.

As myths turned real, the new spirit of theatre social-
ised all it touched. If, as Brecht once satirically remarked, the Germans can make an abstraction even of
materialism, then the English can make even the most
abstract thought concrete. In Osborne's hands a forgotten Spanish Faust play by Lope de Vega turned into *A
Bond Honoured* (1966), where the hero is no longer a
sinner in the hands of God but an ordinary Londoner
with a lower-class accent and manners to match. All that

can be fuelled by personal resentments, as in Arnold
Wesker's *Roots* trilogy (1961), which was based on
memories of an impoverished childhood in Stepney and
rural Norfolk, and resentment can make the choice of
realism look natural, even inevitable, though such social
origins are no humbler than Noël Coward's. Osborne
was a Londoner born in 1929, his father a commercial
artist and his mother a former barmaid; and in his
autobiography, *A Better Class of Person* (1981) he has
cheerfully described the social embarrassments of an
infancy passed between two contrasting worlds, one
middle-class and one lower. Such playwrights exorcise a
sense of early social deprivation, seldom exceptional as
it is, by mythologising it for the public stage, and
Wesker's *Chicken Soup* and Osborne's *Look Back in Anger*
are purgative acts in which early humiliations are lo-
cated, analysed and placed beyond the reach of hurt.

The problems raised in such plays, and only partly
overcome, lie not in their dedication to realism but in
their noisy commitment to dogmas that fail to fit. The
new drama is realistic, and that is its strength. It is also,
less happily, a world of easy theorising, of general
notions quickly adopted and as quickly abandoned, and
that is its weakness. It amply exemplifies Iris Murdoch's
philosophical stricture that all theory ultimately falsifies
and distorts. In the second play of his trilogy, for
example, which is *Roots* (1959), Wesker invites his audience to believe that popular songs are composed out of a
sense of contempt for mass audiences by the moguls
who cynically control the media. But the song he
invents to illustrate that proposition, 'I'll wait for you in
heaven's blue', shows that it is harder to write good or
even passable pop than he imagines, and 1959 was only
a year or two before the advent of the Beatles. The
masses allegedly conditioned out of their minds by the
consumer societies of Western capitalism may not have

been as gullible as he thinks; and the final enlightenment of his heroine, Beatie Bryant, from the mass-
produced and the third-rate on which the play ends –
'I'm talking. . . . I'm not quoting any more' – calls for
more faith than many in the audience can bring to it.
John Arden's *Sergeant Musgrave's Dance*, in the same
year, asks its audience to believe that the failure of a
group of deserters to convert a Victorian mining town to
pacifism is a convincing symbol of the high-minded
endeavours of the modern Left. That, in a way, is all too
true. The play attempts ballad theatre in the manner of
Brecht, but its irrealism of form is no greater than its
irrealism of content, and the notion that all wars are
forced on decent peace-loving folk by sinister Establish-
ments is too silly to be swallowed for an instant,
especially by a people that had just defeated Hitler. The
drab wings of History, Marxist-style, beat earnestly
behind some of these early attempts to characterise the
realities of a post-war world; and the first act of
Osborne's *Look Back* offers a surprisingly old-fashioned
defence of the fading doctrine of class-war. There *was* no
class-war happening outside the Royal Court Theatre
when it opened there in May 1956, and there has been
none since: what the play enacts, when it stops
preaching and starts showing, is not a struggle between
classes but between generations. It is not about upper
and lower but old and young: a social civil war lived out
in words, one way or another, and sometimes bitter
words, behind a good half of the house-fronts in the
land.

It was the creative mistake of the new drama, at the
start, to misdescribe a conflict between youth and age as
a war between a bourgeoisie and a proletariat. It may be
worth asking why that mistake was ever made. A school
of literature, after all, does not need a theory of history
at all. But theory has the advantage of being brief,

modish and portable, and it can seduce for a time. 'We all stand at an open door,' Doris Lessing wrote in *Declaration* (1957), a collection of essays by new and emerging writers edited by Tom Maschler, rhapsodising over 'a new man about to be born, who has never been twisted by drudgery.' The remark is breathtakingly naive. But then a kitten will dart at anything that moves, and the revolutionary dogmas of that age looked as if they were in motion. Marxism was thought to be creative and socialism the way the world was going. Events have long since discredited all that. They have also illustrated that the literary mind is easily deceived into supposing a century-old doctrine to be the latest thing. When Kenneth Tynan, on seeing Brecht's *Mutter Courage* in 1957, told his wife it had made him a Marxist, he had not bothered to discover that the play had been written in 1941 by a German communist during the Nazi-Soviet pact to assist Hitler's war effort. Intellectual addictions to theory can be glib and shallow: ignorant of sources and historical context, and complacently content to remain so.

To dramatise a generation-struggle between the energy of youth and the apathy of parenthood is none the less a potent theatrical idea. *Look Back* was less a political programme, in the end, than a cry for enthusiasm – any enthusiasm. 'There aren't any good, brave causes left,' its hero cries, remembering a father who had died of wounds received in Spain. Jimmy Porter tries to enthuse the shabby attic he shares with a wife, a lodger and eventually a mistress, and his rhetoric is hard-hitting:

Nobody thinks, nobody cares. No beliefs, no convictions and no enthusiasm. Just another Sunday evening,

and he uses first abuse, then infidelity, to break his

wife's will – submissive and unshrewish as she is – and bring her into loving subjection. The play has been charged with providing no sufficient cause for anger, and the reasons Jimmy gives are plainly not those he feels, which belong less to politics than to the marriage-bed. Anger can easily misdescribe itself and mistake its own source, and the chip on Jimmy's shoulder is not an education outside Oxford and Cambridge or even the older civic universities – 'not redbrick but white tile' – or the self-imposed humiliation of running a sweet-stall for a living. It is a sheer excess of spirit: an excess emotionally satisfied, for a time, by his wife's best friend. Tynan greeted the play in a generous hyperbole when he called Jimmy 'the completest young pup in our literature since Hamlet, Prince of Denmark';[3] and Hamlet, too, has been plausibly charged with missing the point of his own confusions of mind. The marriage at the heart of the play has to be destroyed by a vital excess of passion before it can be restored. Kitchen Sink was always more than a realism of stage-sets. At its best, it was a realism of the heart, where the dream-figures that had inhabited the verse-dramas of Eliot and Fry have yielded place to beings that give back to audiences a telling reflection of their own anxieties and unspoken longings.

★   ★   ★

Tynan's famous hyperbole about *Look Back* and *Hamlet*, however, is only part true of the revival of a tradition, and Osborne's real sources were not Shakespeare but something much nearer his own time.

If the traditional strength of British fiction is comic realism, then *Look Back* is a traditional play, and its real sources are in Sheridan, Wilde and Coward. For two centuries and more there has been an unappeasable need for prose comedies on the London stage, new or revived, and no verse drama can satisfy that hunger. Political radicalism is not the point. Real people talk prose, and one likes to laugh at oneself and one's own. Osborne, in any case, was to turn conservative at an accelerating pace in the 1960s, when a new wave of youthful radicalism rapidly threatened his own. Radical noises in those days were supposed to be for the young, and the long diatribe against youth in *Inadmissible Evidence* (1965), which followed *Look Back* by less than a decade, suggests that public affairs always concerned the dramatist less as a programme than as an area of debate in which to strike attitudes that define, to others and to oneself, one's own place in the world:

> Nothing, certainly not your swinging distaste, can match what I feel for you. . . . There is no lather or fear in you, all cool, dreamy, young, cool and not a proper blemish, forthright, unimpressed, contemptuous of ambition but good and pushy all the same. You've no shame of what you are . . . No one before has been able to do such things with such charm, such ease, such frozen innocence as all of you seem to have, to me . . .

That sounds like the envy of those who have suffered for a generation which, as they suppose, has not. It is a fervent case for the bad old days: a new-found conservatism extended, as a case, in *West of Suez* (1971), which comments on the decolonisation of Africa and the West Indies only a decade after it happened. The hero of that play is not a youth like Jimmy Porter but an elderly author called Wyatt Gillman, a creature wholly British in being at once absurd and wittily conscious of his own absurdity: a hero of disillusion who utters scathingly conservative views about the world around him. The

play broke new ground, among writers freshly minted
since the war, in suggesting subversively that it might
be possible to be conservative and intelligent at the
same time – a hypothesis as disturbing to theatre
audiences as anything anywhere proposed in *Look Back*.
When Gillman is summarily killed at the end of the play
by local nationalists, someone exclaims 'My God,
they've shot the fox!', and the symbolism is blunt. That
old quarry for radicals known as the British Empire,
happily hunted for as long as anyone could remember,
was suddenly noticed to be dead, and progressives felt
suddenly naked in the need for a better argument. They
had lost their best game. Their fox was dead: killed off,
in the worst of bad form, around 1960 by a Conservative
government.

★   ★   ★

Osborne's theatrical realism was never wholly political;
and it was impelled from the start, like Amis's fiction, by
a passion for social manners and a fascination with
social taboos. The hero of *Look Back* had been an
implacable critic of word, gesture and conduct – a
carping conoisseur of everyone's behaviour except his
own. A stage-direction speaks of his 'blistering honesty
or apparent honesty' and of his tenderness and
freebooting cruelty, which suggests that, like Hamlet, he
embraces opposites. The play is not just a tract in
support of his case. It excites pity as well as assent. The
first act, by far the best, is a scintillating diatribe against
the manners and morals of the age, and it marks a
theatrical return. After the brief digression of poetic
drama, British theatre reverts here to a tradition a
century and more old, and the mid-century Kitchen
Sink school can plausibly claim a dramatic ancestry that
is continuously longer than any other. An emphasis on

abuse, contention and social banter in dramatic dialogue is the tradition of Shakespeare's *Much Ado*, after all, and of Congreve, Sheridan and Shaw. It is a tradition of theatre that cannot easily die, since it gratifies audiences with the sight and sound of a world they intimately know.

The limitations remain. A master of mannerism, Osborne was never a master of construction, and knew it. *Look Back* had fumbled for an ending; and the end it gets, fiercely anti-feminine in an age between feminisms, shows a returned wife grovelling for forgiveness and nestling in her husband's arms in a childish whimsy about squirrels and bears. That has nothing to do with class-war or generation-war, and it is a highly wishful contribution to the literary battle of the sexes. But then starting one play and ending another is the characteristic mode of this playwright, and his plots are often a mass of loose ends, committing such outrageously deliberate mistakes, at times, as forgetting a character after the first act or creating an expectancy for one that never appears. Osborne's disdain for construction is candid. 'If I would never make it as a theatrical draughtsman,' he remarks in his memoir, on reading Pinero in youth, 'I could never be so dull either,' recalling his contempt on hearing an agent recommend 'the Newtonian principle of theatre' embodied in Rattigan's *Winslow Boy*. All that suggests an open defiance of the Well-Made Play, even a defiant proclamation of the Ill-Made Play. Coward on Construction, he decided when young, looked 'pretty wobbly'. All of which is as presumptuous as Jimmy Porter, since the Kitchen Sink owed more to Coward and his kind than it was ever ready to confess. Above all, it owed the concept of the dramatic quartet.

The dramatic quartet is a foursome of lovers who change partners, whether temporarily or permanently, like the four lovers in Shakespeare's *A Midsummer*

Night's Dream or the two married couples in Ford Madox
Ford's *The Good Soldier* (1915). Coward deftly re-adapted
it to comic theatre in *Private Lives* (1930), where the
crisscross of married couples is completed, one is meant
to guess, shortly after the end of the play: as Elyot and
Amanda steal off to resume their interrupted marriage,
their second spouses, deserted on their wedding-nights,
fall into that irritable quarrelling which in Coward
betokens love. *Look Back* is a kitchen-sink version of
Private Lives – a broken marriage resumed after a bout of
bickering and adultery – though here the crisscross is
unmatched by any rival pair. It is no blunter than
Coward, who was also a master of verbal abuse. It is
Coward in the attic.

Coward's plays, at their best, were nothing like wobbly in construction. They were to be revived shortly
before his death in 1973, when a fashion for theatrical
squalor was replaced, in its turn, by a revived taste for
elegance and wit. Since then he has grown in stature
both as a dramatist and a song-writer, and it is hard to
think of any other playwright of the century who has
left four comedies – the last of the four, *Present Laughter*,
appeared in 1942 – that are forever revivable. His
post-war achievements in theatre were admittedly anti-
climactic, but the Kitchen Sink owed him more than it
was ever ready to concede; more, too, than he, in his
horror of the new style, would ever have wished to
acknowledge. Even their faults resemble his. Coward
could write brittle dialogue, Osborne brittle diatribe, till
the cows come home, and both were good haters. What
they lack, and what their successors Pinter and Stoppard often lack, is the supreme dramatic talent of
making things happen on stage: happen, as opposed to
being recollected, explained or foretold. Their inventive
powers lie with words rather than with events, and their
plays sometimes show the strain of too large a depend-

ence on sheer talk. Stoppard once remarked in a lecture: 'I know what I want to say – the problem is: who says it?', adding that characters can all too easily be walking statements: 'I like stereotypes, and would like to write a play of nothing but.' Flesh and blood does not come naturally to this school of dramatists. Coward's usual device for stretching the action had been to compose a comic cameo for a menial, like the breakfast-serving French maid in the last act of *Private Lives*. In Osborne and in his successors, much of the action occurs off-stage, to be described in long retrospective speeches. Simon Gray's *The Common Pursuit* (1984) is an extreme instance of that awkward theatrical device. The new dramatist is undeniably a master of language, and he has chosen drama rather than fiction, it may be supposed, because he loves theatre and above all dialogue. But he is less clearly a master of action, and the two-hour traffic of the stage is sometimes visibly too long for him.

★　　★　　★

With Harold Pinter, born a year after Osborne, construction is everything, and the dramatic trio replaces the quartet.

Pinter is the classic dramatist of the threesome, which includes above all the love-triangle. Starting as an actor, like Osborne, his first full-length West End play, *The Birthday Party*, failed in 1958 after short runs in Oxford and Cambridge; and his triumph was delayed for another two years, when *The Caretaker* (1960) was justly greeted with critical acclaim. If Osborne was the emerging dramatist of the 1950s, soon to be eclipsed, then it was Pinter in the 1960s who eclipsed him. Triumphantly a master of construction, and never wobbly, his plays are as taut as Osborne's are loose. In fact they hang in air, as one watches, or in the memory as one recalls, like the dry lines that compose the diagrams of a geometrician; and his masterly distillation of Proust's seven novels, *The Proust Screenplay* (1978), though still unmade as a film, shows how he can command essentials and pare to the bone.

That passion for abstraction is unavowed, even denied, and Pinter's own declarations about his art, whether in private or in public, seem as often designed to evade as to enlighten. 'Everything to do with the play is in the play,' he once told his director, Peter Wood, speaking of *The Birthday Party*.[4] Eight years later, and suddenly famous, his reticence was unaltered: 'I had – I have – nothing to say about myself, directly.'[5] 'I'm no theoretician,' he told a BBC interviewer in 1971. 'I just like the sniff of words on the page.' But if theoreticians are people who have theories, then he is surely among them: the real question about him, at times, and the real doubt, being whether he is anything else. His characters are commonly unfleshed, but his plays are eminently explainable, however prudent it may be to leave the explaining to others. Perhaps the critics who killed *The Birthday Party* in London in 1958 were right to complain that its single point was too small, and too deeply buried, to be worth digging hard for. But the play is not ultimately unclear, and its theme of nameless menace has been succinctly anatomised by Pinter himself in a brief poem called 'A View of the Party'. *The Caretaker* is a work of arresting clarity. It presents, in the starkest dramaturgical simplicity, a tramp called Davies and two brothers, one cruel and the other kind; and in an elegantly wrought study in ingratitude, Davies respects the cruel brother and despises the kind. The care he takes, and that they take, is of more than one kind, and in the end he is taken care of by the folly of his own choice. This is a play that cries out to be interpreted, even if the dramatist himself has always declined to be his own interpreter. Terence Rattigan, thinking he had understood it, once explained to Pinter that the cruel brother is the God of the Old Testament and the kind one the God of the New, with Davies as Man himself; but Pinter, true to form, merely looked puzzled, it is said, and replied: 'It's about a caretaker and two brothers.'

Pinter's mind is starkly and startlingly theoretical, as dramatists go: doubly so, one is tempted to add, as British dramatists go. He is as much a theorist of the stage as Brecht or Beckett. Born in London in 1930, the son of a poor Jewish tailor, he was educated at Hackney grammar school by a highly gifted Cambridge-educated teacher of English, and went on to a drama school rather than to a university because he did not have enough Latin to try for Oxford or Cambridge and had never, as he tells, heard of any other university; to become, for several years, a travelling actor. Like many others who have never tasted higher education, he may be inclined to demand of theories and generalities more than they properly have to give. But his mind has always been given to abstraction and highly receptive to moral principle. Pacifism, after all, is that, and he was a conscientious objector to military service as a teenager in 1948–9. Echoes of great issues abound in the tinkle of trivial domestic details out of which his plays are built. The landlady's naive boast about her seaside boarding-house in *The Birthday Party* – 'we're on the list' – can hardly avoid echoing the memory of Nazi extermina-tions of the 1940s, since the play ends with a brutal interrogation and the abduction of its hero to an un-known fate. Pinter artfully distracts the mind from that over-evident interpretation, like an abstract painter an-xious that his brush might inadvertently represent something real, by making one of the interrogators, and not the hero, a Jew; but that, no doubt, is just his tease. The suave elegance of *The Caretaker*, again, at once brutal and refined, is founded on a triangular design that has all the fascination of a logical puzzle or Rubik's cube: it is a moral fable about ingratitude and power worship. *The Homecoming* (1965), perhaps his greatest play and among his most ruthless, implicitly asks what a familiar human world would be like if men were capable of lust but never of love; and when the profession of Ruth, the new daughter-in-law, is successively revealed to her male relatives – she is a former prostitute ready to return to her trade – they compete for her favours like jungle beasts. *Old Times*, which opened six years later in 1971, asks whether one can be said to remember events that never occurred – a question once famously engaged upon by Bertrand Russell and G. E. Moore[6] – and shows three old friends reminiscing about a remote past and creating fictions out of their lives even as they strive to recall them. *No Man's Land* (1975) imagines a world in which the familiar conversational device of tactfully changing the subject – a convention utterly fundamental to British traditions of everyday courtesy – has been miraculously abolished, so that the play leaves the characters, still striving to appear polite, forever locked within a topic they have unfortunately begun. And *Betrayal* (1978) describes a triangle of adultery backwards, starting with the final estrangement of the lovers and ending where the action began, in a seduction; so that the audience views events not as the characters have lived them but like historians, in full knowledge of the outcome. Life is lived forwards but remembered backwards, and the play reminds that we interpret by over-interpreting – our own lives, and others – after having lived them.

The advanced technique at work here deserves a name, even if a name has to be invented; and the name might be Subtracted Realism. By Subtracted Realism I mean some utterly ordinary slice of social reality – usually, in this case, Pinter's London – with one element of the real subtracted like a piece of cake, so that it is noticed not by its presence but by its absence. When a cake lacks a single segment, no one doubts where it once was or what it was made of. Human situations, in a similar way, can be significant by virtue of what they omit. If there could be loveless human creatures for whom desire was exclusively carnal, then they might be the characters of *The Homecoming* – more like beasts than men. If human beings could strive so hard to recall without recalling, they might be like those in *Old Times*. If a husband could divide his two traditional functions of breadwinner and lover, he might behave like the hero of that artful little television play *The Lover* (1963), who returns from the office after a breakfast signal from his wife – 'Is your lover coming today?' he asks her brightly, and she murmurs agreement – to make love under the kitchen table as the third element in a sort of triangle-for-two. Trios like these, lucidly geometrical as they are, are plainly the outcome of a lively theoretical curiosity that has perceived a new possibility within realism: as new as anything Beckett, pioneer of the new theoretical minimalism, ever saw. This is a drama that scores by omission. But then *Hamlet* without the prince, as a rival playwright was about to show, might make one think quite hard about Hamlet.

Three-sided plays like these grow out of glimpsing at a new set of rules – a new geometry – in the old game of realism. Reality is not static. The milieux of Pinter's plays have risen, as he has risen, from the grim realities of the East End to the grim-in-another-way world of the fashionable West End, where poverty is replaced by torturing doubts about status and fidelity. No realism is ever unqualified. 'What goes on in my plays is realistic,'

Pinter himself has written in an introduction to his *Plays: Two* (1977), 'but what I'm doing is not realism.' The remark suggests a far more deliberate intelligence than just sniffing words on the page. This is the theatre of a subtle and unrelenting critical mind musing on the greatest of all social paradoxes of twentieth-century Britain: that though conversation exists to disguise meaning as well as to reveal it, no one can fail in some measure to communicate when he speaks. Speech reveals far more, in this theatre of words, than its characters wish; and we communicate not too little, as some believe, but all too much. The game of social living, in this view, is a little like a game of chess, where no player ever yields up a piece willingly but only under the iron rules of the game, and preferably as part of an exchange with a rival: nothing for nothing.

Pinterian dialogue is a remorseless game of skill, and revelations abound even in the most conventional remarks. 'As it is?', one character asks of another at the opening of *No Man's Land*, holding out a glass; and it is utterly plain from the phrase that he is the host and that the home he entertains in is socially a cut above Hackney. That is a lot of information for three words. But then even the most commonplace remark can be rank-defining and class-bound, and speech betrays everyone who uses it by its inherent lack of privacy. Even at its most conventional it is endlessly, hopelessly, betrayingly significant.

★   ★   ★

Tom Stoppard, who represents the new theatre of the 1970s as plainly as Osborne and Pinter once represented the preceding decades, was born in Czechoslovakia in 1937 and brought up in Singapore and India, later England; to become a Bristol journalist and achieve stage success in 1966 with a play that is literally *Hamlet* without the prince. It is called *Rosencrantz and Guildenstern Are Dead*, and with *Jumpers* (1972) and *Travesties* (1974) he established, and before the age of forty, a reputation in London theatre inferior to none: a name confirmed by *Night and Day* (1978) and *Hapgood* (1988). This was a triumph of opposition. Stoppard may have taken fire from James Saunders's *Next Time I'll Sing to You*, which opened in the West End, to critical acclaim, in 1963, and he studied drama in West Berlin with Saunders shortly after; but he is as playful as his predecessors were anguished, as irreverent as they were grim. His success, like Saunders's, represents a revival of a rococo mood among British audiences, tired and tamed in spirit by the kitchen-sink school and its thin-blooded successors; prosperous, too, at long last, mostly by their own enterprise, and suddenly unashamed of worldly success. With Saunders and Stoppard, in the mid 1960s, serious drama regained its comic face.

Rosencrantz and Guildenstern opened at the Edinburgh Festival in 1966, performed on the fringe by the Oxford Drama Group, and it dealt with chance and probability as a set of logical puzzles and Wittgensteinian language-games. This was philosophy tamed to the living-room: it was also a famous fiction – the most famous tragedy in the language – turned inside-out. A fascination with the inside-out seems to have belonged to the mood of the moment. A patchwork quilt, if reversed, can look oddly interesting, even if it was never meant to be seen from that side, and Stoppard's play was about the action of *Hamlet* seen from the wrong side: the standpoint of two near-nonentities in Shakespeare's drama. By a happy coincidence it appeared in the same year as Jean Rhys's novel *The Wide Sargasso Sea* (1966), which re-imagined Charlotte Brontë's *Jane Eyre* from the standpoint of Mr Rochester's first, mad wife. Masterpieces exist to be

interrogated, even rewritten, and a fascination with
narrative points of view makes for a mood where
philosophy and literature meet. *Jumpers*, six years later,
was an utterly unsubversive satire on academic philosophy from the pen of someone who was never a student,
though endowed with a journalist's quick grasp of
materials. But this is a dramatist whose vocation ultimately lay with contemporary or near-contemporary
history, uniting journalistic skills and comic turns that
belong not far from the end of the pier. History, as he
soon discovered, though dangerous, is also funny:
recent history can easily be dangerous and funny at the
same time.

Again, interviews can mislead. 'I burn with no
causes,' Stoppard once told a newspaper: 'I cannot say
that I write with any social objective. One writes because one loves writing.'[7] But like Pinter's disclaimers,
that is to be tested and not swallowed. Stoppard's plays,
especially his later plays, bristle with lively and subversive political points. *Travesties* is built up as a series of
rapid contrasts, like a succession of music-hall turns,
mainly between James Joyce and Lenin – a writer and a
man of action – based on the happy accident that they
both lived in Zurich during the first World War: the one
writing *Ulysses*, the other preparing a revolution. The
play is unremittingly playful; it was also, for 1974,
iconoclastic. In an intellectual atmosphere still emerging, but not yet quite emerged, from the fashionable
Marxism of the previous decade, its brash handling of
Lenin looked breezily and daringly irreverent, a sort of
bold anti-canonisation. Nor is it likely to be unmotivated
that the play appeared shortly after the military occupation of Czechoslovakia by the successors of Lenin in
1968. Since *Travesties* Stoppard has been suspect among
the leftovers of the New Left as intellectually unreliable
and hopelessly frivolous, a lighthearted blasphemer

against the God of progress: charges as serious as any to
be made. Where Osborne turned conservative and Pinter grew sceptical of traditional socialism, Stoppard was
and remained a liberal, his abiding fascination being
with individual mind and its liberties under law. His
vision is humanistic, where the individual embodies the
human species in all its contradictions. Every Rosencrantz has a Hamlet in him, as every dullard yearns at
times to be a hero, and every Hamlet a Rosencrantz;
every Joyce a Lenin, every Lenin a Joyce, as thinking
and acting beings are ultimately and in their inner
natures all one. We live our lives as doubles, he argues
in *Hapgood*: 'the priest is visited by the doubter, the
Marxist sees the civilising force of the bourgeoisie, the
captain of industry admits the justice of common own-
ership.' That leaves class-war and race-war nowhere;
and *Night and Day* (1978), which is set in a new African
dictatorship, argued ingeniously for freedom of the
press against those who think newspapers no more
than a millionaire's racket: 'People don't buy rich men's
papers because the men are rich: the men are rich
because people buy their papers'; and a state where
'only a particular approved, licensed, and supervised
non-millionaire can have a newspaper is called, for
example, Russia.'

With this dramatist the comic turn suddenly looked
lethal. Even *The Real Thing* (1982), though almost pure
comedy of manners, includes some hefty derision of
left-wing demonstrators and their self-indulgent view of
art as an act of self-expression for which others should
be forced to pay; and *Professional Foul* (1977), perhaps
the best television play yet written in English expressly
for that medium, is a highly serious comedy about the
communist oppression of Stoppard's native land.

Stoppard might be called an historical dramatist, then,
in the highly special sense in which a journalist is an

historian. He writes of events that have only recently occurred and with a sharp sense of their immediate causation and context. His first play in that mode, *Travesties*, represents a powerful kick-start to a vogue that has since proved irresistible to playwrights and audiences. Theatre-audiences, like novel-readers, love to be taught: knowledge, after all, is entertaining as well as useful. Since the 1970s contemporary and near-contemporary history has become the chief flavour of London theatre – with an occasional return to a remoter past, as in Peter Shaffer's Mozart play *Amadeus* (1980), which in a success-mad age was a plea for the dignity of mediocrity. The stuff of theatre is now on the library shelf. There has been a play about Stalin bullying two Soviet composers in the Kremlin in 1946 – David Pownall's *Master Class* (1983); another about T. S. Eliot's first, tragic marriage – Michael Hastings's *Tom and Viv* (1985); another about refugees in war-time Hollywood, Christopher Hampton's *Tales from Hollywood* (1983); and a flood of plays about those who spied for Russia and how they were recruited, spurred by a ministerial announcement in the House of Commons in 1979 that Anthony Blunt, Surveyor of the Queen's Paintings, had been a Soviet spy. Julian Mitchell's *Another Country* (1981), for example, set in a public school, is plainly an echo of that affair, and it deals with the link between treason and homosexuality in a privileged class before the war. Hugh Whitmore's *Pack of Lies* (1982) is about another spy, or pair of spies; Alan Bennett's *The Old Country* (1978) shows one of them settled in the Soviet Union, and his *Single Spies* (1989) returns, and explicitly, to Blunt. That is no more than a handful of instances among many. In the years around 1590 Marlowe and Shakespeare turned to the Plantagenets as a subject for the stage, and between them invented the chronicle play; in the 1970s London theatre, once again, turned to chronicling – to a recent, half-remembered and controversial past. Fiction, as someone once said, can easily turn into faction: it can present not just the realistic but the real.

So large a shift of emphasis needs to be explained, and two explanations may be provisionally submitted. One is that dramatists love to work in existing materials, much as sculptors do; and a biography or a cache of manuscripts – even a prime minister's statement from a dispatch box – may be the playwright's block of marble. It gives you somewhere to start. The other is that audiences may easily prefer actions that are linked, however tenuously, to real events. They fear they may have missed something. History, after all, is a great explainer, especially recent history, and the world one has to understand if it is to be lived in at all can be explained by theatre as well as by newspapers and novels. Plays can even offer instant history: there was a sort of play about the Falklands war of 1982, when the Falkland Islands were forcibly repossessed by a British task force, on the upstairs boards of the Royal Court theatre within months of the South Atlantic crisis itself. Called *Falkland Sound*, it was little more than a collage of documents and letters: which may suggest either haste, or a love of authenticity, or both.

No one can complain that British theatre in recent times has failed to meet Hamlet's call to hold a mirror to nature and reflect the age. Theatre is not a fairyland, a playground or a wish-fulfilling dream. It is a record of history. Hamlet called actors the abstract and brief chronicles of the time, meaning that they summarise and interpret the confusions of the real world, actual and remembered. They are, if not literally necessary, wanted. History, in any case, is not dull; and the London stage, serious of purpose as it often is, has not ceased to entertain: in fact Stoppard is a more amusing fellow than Osborne or Pinter, and knows that historical interpretation can be a romp, if you let it. It is rather that the amorous play of the fictional trio or quartet is no longer felt to be enough. In a world avid to know itself and its past, theatre has entered eagerly into the didactic spirit of its age and become a teacher.

8

The Battle of the Sexes

Class there has always been to divide mankind, and the Victorians added race. The 1950s rediscovered the battle-ground of sex: a battle which, though familiar to ancient and medieval mankind, had been largely abandoned as a literary theme between the world wars.

The discovery, or recovery, was not feministic. Feminism is a fashion that comes and goes in waves. It was known to the Victorians and, in the years before 1914, it mounted the noisiest of all public campaigns of the day, the suffragette movement. The new wave that began in 1968 in New York, soon to be known as the Women's Movement, was late, derivative and imitative. By then the male author had drawn up the lines of battle and opened his attack, in plays, novels and elsewhere, on the female of the species: John Osborne's *Look Back in Anger* (1956), a radical play that knows a lot about protest-movements but nothing, apparently, about feminism, is bitterly and provocatively anti-woman; and anti-woman diatribes, old as the Ancients as a literary topic – Juvenal's sixth satire is the classic statement in Latin – echo largely unanswered through the 1950s and after. John Fowles's *Mantissa* (1982) is a novel designed, perhaps, as no more than a footnote to his major fiction, since a mantissa is a modest addition or appendix, but it cheekily demands to know why it is that women always want talk as well as sex – the hero concluding that they have invented literature as a revenge on the male:

to get their own back, deliberately to confuse and

175

distract their masculine betters; to make them waste
their vital intellectual aspirations and juices on man-
tissae and trivia,

the Women's Movement being pretentious ninnery and
no more than an elaborate device for getting what they
want. (And what they want is always the same thing.)
That is straight out of Juvenal or Chaucer, as a point,
though at least it tips a nod and a wink towards recent
protest-movements. Kingsley Amis's *Stanley and the
Women* (1984), similarly, is a novel fiercely male in its
loyalties, and it pays scant attention to the Women's
Movement, which surfaces as nothing more interesting
than a new tactic in an age-old game between the sexes
of dominate-or-be-dominated, kill-or-be-killed. An earlier Amis novel, *Jake's Thing* (1978), had gloomily suggested that middle-aged impotence might even be seen
as an advantage, and Jake ends by accepting a sexless
Oxford life in a place just about to yield itself up to
co-residence. You do not need feminism, in fact, to have
a Cold War between the sexes, and the 1960s feminist
can reasonably claim that men had started it all.

Male abuse of womankind, what is more, can be
extreme. Women are like Russians, a character in Amis's
Stanley remarks:

If you did exactly what they wanted, all the time, you
were being realistic and constructive and promoting
the cause of peace – and if you ever stood up to them,
you were resorting to cold-war tactics and pursuing
imperialistic designs and interfering in their internal
affairs, (ch. 2)

so that the peace-loving male can easily end up in the
posture of Finland. Strong stuff, and much in the
tradition of Juvenal's classic satire, where ladies of rank,

spendthrift and quarrelsome, work in the stews for fun and riotously spend their husbands' fortune while caring nothing about joining them at work. It is easy, even for feminists, to forget that in the literary battle of the sexes war was long ago declared by the male.

Osborne's first produced play is a case in point. *Look Back* was hostile to wealth and age as well as to women; but his hostility to women, as a species, was to remain something like a constant in his writings after other hatreds had faded. Jimmy Porter calls his submissive wife pusillanimous, openly invoking an ancient tradition of male abuse:

> It sounds like some fleshy Roman matron, doesn't it? The Lady Pusillanimous seen here with her husband Sextus, on their way to the Games. Poor old Sextus. . . . Pusillanimous. Adjective. Wanting of firmness of mind, of small courage, having a little mind, mean-spirited, cowardly, timid of mind. That's my wife. . . .

So womankind is feeble-minded if constant, like Jimmy's wife, and worse if not. She is allowed to support her man at board and in bed, in return for disdain or abuse; to work outside the home to service the family debt; and to perform when required the one act she can uniquely perform, which is to conceive and bear children. Her inferiority, in that view, is a fact of nature, not the fault of man; and no extension of the suffrage, no concessions of courtesy or compliment-paying, can alter it. The lines are drawn.

★   ★   ★

The new wave of feminism in the late 1960s uncritically accepted many of these assumptions, and without noticing how much it had accepted. Germaine Greer's

Female Eunuch (1970), the first book of an Australian-
born Cambridge graduate, opened its case as a renewed
declaration of war by 'the second feminist wave': the
first wave, the Suffragettes, having won their battle for
the vote and then given up, as she believed, since they
had failed to enter the professions or use their votes to
any concerted effect. The book is written with garrulous
gusto, and it openly acknowledges its origins in the
New Left of the late 1960s and its conventional views,
with 'revolution' as a bravo-word; in fact it is confidently dedicated, in routine Marxist terms, to 'the coming
classless society and the withering away of the state'.
That was in 1970. Then the world changed, and towards
neither. By 1984, with its sequel *Sex and Destiny*, neither
classlessness nor the withering of the state looked
imminent, so that *The Female Eunuch* is now a book
intriguingly marooned by history, its assumptions distant in time and often demolished, as the author herself
has conceded, by the forward march of events.

If such books are a polemical answer to Amis and
Osborne, then it is notable how much the two sides
have in common as products of a time and a place. As
socialists (or ex-socialists) they take it for granted that
conflict, not stability or cooperation, is the natural
source of all progress. Again, they are ardently success-
worshipping. Amis's Lucky Jim and Osborne's Jimmy
ardently seek worldly success and hotly envy those who
have more of it; and Lucky Jim, at least, may be
presumed to get it: at least he goes off, on the last page
of the novel, to what sounds like a promising job in the
money-market. *The Female Eunuch* is careerist in a similar
sense: it boasts of women who have made it in a man's
world, and calls for more of them: 'the first woman
judge', 'her own brokerage firm' ... All that sounds
more like praise for capitalism than for Marxist revolution, and one is left wondering what place brokerage

would play in a classless society. The real question here
– an extra-literary one – is why work, once seen as
tedious and demeaning, and not least by ladies of rank,
so suddenly acquired status, and why cultivated leisure
so suddenly and so totally lost it.

Sex and Destiny is even more conservative than that,
and it praises, of all things, the patriarchal values of
Italian peasant life. Hardly radical at all, now, except in
being anti-rich, it is sceptical of family planning as a
world solution and convinced that in the end traditional
social values are best. 'I stopped trying to shock the
peasantry,' Greer wrote of her time in southern Italy –
accepting their ancient village morality, sterner than any
priest's, as something noble and profound – 'and sued
instead for acceptance by the other women.' Suing for
acceptance is crucial to second-phase feminism, which
has proved conformist in a way the suffragette movement never was. This is not an attempt to change a
system but a bid to join it.

The literature of feminism, in its 1960s phase, has
proved itself a literature obsessed with social acceptance. It based itself on the unshaken assumption that
what the world esteems is rank, promotion and wealth,
and its early hostility to riches was plainly no more than
provisional and short-term. Left was never radical, it is
now clear, and these are highly unradical books. They
seek not to change the total nature of society, that is, but
to grab a bigger share of it by rising through the existing
hierarchies. The system, one feels, has little to fear from
the new female sage: her real concern is about her own
slice of the cake. The point is not usually taken. Feminists are so busy condemning gender-stereotyping and
thinking in received categories that they seldom notice
how stereotyped their own notions are, how readily
their own categories have been borrowed from others.
On their own admission, they did not invent feminism

themselves. Like Marxism, it existed before their grand-parents were born.

One of those assumptions concerns the natural role of the male. It is a paradox of the literary battle of the sexes that male writers like Amis and Osborne have portrayed man in his essential ruthlessness and selfishness with a more withering accuracy than any feminist would dare or wish to do. To call Lucky Jim, or Jimmy Porter, a male chauvinist pig would be to understate his confidence in his own natural superiority. The domestic pig, at least, is a largely non-violent animal who, nothing worse than passively selfish, is content to eat and sleep. Jim and Jimmy, by contrast, are artists in emotional terrorism. They demand, as D. H. Lawrence's heroes sometimes did, the mental subjection of a woman as well as her body, like sexual totalitarians; they scheme or scream till they get it; and when they get it, they appear to be confident in having asserted an accepted fact of nature and not just an arrangement self-evidently convenient to themselves. That brutal claim about the nature of the sexes is not questioned in *The Female Eunuch*, and it is largely accepted in *Sex and Destiny*. Women are claimants or suppliants for favours in these texts, and content to remain so. There are no henpecked husbands in the world of the feminist imagination, no matrons quietly confident of ruling their husbands and children in the natural dignity of wife and mother, no women who take professional success so easily for granted that they need to pay no attention either to the Women's Movement or its adversaries. The tunnel is stared through from one end or another, but a tunnel-vision is all it can give, and the wider world of social reality passes unnoticed by both sides of the dispute. The sex-battle of Amis, Osborne and Greer was fought out exclusively within the assumptions of a competitive economy and a race for money and status, and the values of ancient title and gentility of manners – of leisured ease – counted for nothing here. They might not exist. The feminist and anti-feminist alike accepts the jungle, and wants it. And neither has bothered to notice that career-women, in an age in which most of those in jobs are women, are an advantage to the male, whose standard of living would decline catastrophically if women stopped going out to work.

★   ★   ★

The richest literary vein here, in all likelihood, in the battle of the sexes has been mutual non-comprehension.

In a highly competitive age, the spokesmen of the sexes have found it hard and ever harder to understand each other, to know what the other likes or does not like. This is a battle based on a series of defiant misunderstandings. The 1960s feminist believed that men would take womankind more seriously if she were a professional, and above all if she rose high in her profession: unaware, apparently, that the sophisticated skills of a wife and mother can easily seem more mysterious and wonderful to the male than promotion in office or classroom. She believed, too, that her verbal abuse of the male had told the world the worst about him, whereas the worst was far worse than she could imagine or tell; and when the worst is told, or some of it, by male writers, it is dismissed by feminists as irony. The case against men was always stronger than the feminist knew, and the phrase 'male chauvinist pig' imputes nothing worse than selfishness, one of the mildest of the vices. Rapists are male, to be sure, but so are soccer hooligans and lager louts: male violence can be mindless and purposeless. The male, for his part, as Amis's *Stanley and the Women* suggests, can encourage

himself to believe that women are conspiring to drive
men mad unless they get their own way – all of it, and at
once – and that they are involved in a conspiracy
organised by an age-old technique called 'sorting a man
out'. In fact *Stanley* toys earnestly with the hypothesis
that all women, being already mad, are determined to
make men as mad as themselves – an impressive
version of paranoia – but settles reluctantly into the
more moderate hypothesis that they are coolly calculat-
ing beings engaged in a collective conspiracy to pretend
to insanity, or anything, if it will get them what they
want. 'Mad people are confused, adrift, troubled, even
frightened – what woman is?' a character authoritatively
remarks. Quite a lot, probably, though it is beyond the
tolerance of this novelist to imagine it.

All that, as a total theory of the sex-war, is at once
compelling and implausible. *Stanley* asks the reader to
forget something every observant reader must easily
have noticed for himself: that some women, and
perhaps most, like men at least as much as they like
women, and admire them even when they do not like
them. To complete the cycle of fruitful misunderstanding, at least one feminist reviewer greeted the novel as a
work of radical irony and a telling exposure of male
unreason, unable to believe that the author could
seriously share the views of his own hero.

*   *   *

If the new battle of the sexes has shown each side
unreliable about the other, it has shown them, too, less
than utterly reliable about their own.

To the Marxist tradition, in its heyday, conflict was
the foundation-stone of all history and the source of
progress; and conflict was not personal but a matter of
vast generalised forces. It was natural, in such an

atmosphere, that the disputants should find it difficult to accept that man might differ from man as well as from woman, or woman from woman – as worker, in reality, differs from worker or bourgeois from bourgeois. The 1960s wave of feminists resolved that women must fight their way through the world as members of a single class of beings, as 'sisters': living their lives, speaking their minds, choosing their sexual partners, defending themselves boldly against violation and deciding whether or not to bear children; and the period before 1968 was dubbed a period of low consciousness. They declined to notice, unlike the author of *Stanley and the Women*, that women, like men, had techniques for getting their own way long before feminism was thought of, and that you do not have to be a feminist, or a woman, to be against rape. The masculine propagandist could be as partial as the feminist, and as unrepresentative of his sex. In the fictions of Amis and Osborne the male, if still in active life, is a being perpetually on heat, drowning his desire in rhetoric or alcohol, or both; and anyone who finds it easy, or even possible, to get along without women is a wimp or a pervert. The battle, once joined, was remarkably balanced. This was a dispute between rival obsessives who always shared far more than they ever wished to notice, and who chose to look at the real world less candidly than they claimed. The assumption that sex is the main determinant of human behaviour is after all nothing like self-evident; the claim that if it is not that, then it should be, mere special pleading. The post-war world is full of people who live alone because they like it; others cohabit, by choice, in passionless amity. That is not a principled monasticism. Privacy has its charms and its practical uses, and for some natures chastity is natural, comfortable and unenforced.

Another shared assumption is there only by omission,

and it concerns an implicit admiration of male virtues –
virtues, that is, traditionally associated with men. The
second feminist wave that began in 1968 was about
making women more like men, or at least more like
career-men: active rather than supportive, that is, initiating rather than merely responsive, vital and creative. Nobody suggested that the world might be better if
men – or at least some men – tried to become more like
women. The feminist was at least as male in her loyalties
as any man; the male found it all the easier, for that
reason, to charge her with calculation and fraud. Both
sides have since come to look partial and incoherent.
Both had failed to consider that women might have as
much to teach men, in the search for wisdom and virtue,
as men could ever teach women.

The terminology of the battle of the sexes, if coolly
pondered, reveals an interesting omission. There is a
word for the imitation of men by women, and that word
is feminism. There is none for the imitation of women
by men. Masculinism is a term still waiting to be
invented. But then there is no such thing as masculinism, or likely to be. It is unlikely, no doubt, because
many women, in their capacity for compassion and
trust, set too high a standard of virtue for any man to
aspire to with any realistic hope of success. It is so, too,
because no one – man or woman – seriously *wants* to be
as admirable as that if not already so. Florence Nighting-
ale did not make herself virtuous but was. The sexes
have not grown more alike since 1968, and in their
hearts they know they cannot. The battle of the sexes, in
the end, was a battle no one could win, and much of the
literary debate now looks like an exchange in a phoney
war. For men and women do not merely need each
other. They like each other. They are locked into post-
ures of admiration and blank, uncomprehending envy.
How can women be so ministering, so angelic? How can

men be so self-sufficient, so uncaring, so efficiently egotistical? Why do women cry at weddings while their husbands merely wonder in secret whether the champagne was better at the last one?

These are questions to tax the consciences of poets, playwrights and novelists down the decades. In a present-tense novel called *Family and Friends* (1985), for example, Anita Brookner, who is no feminist, has wonderingly portrayed the phenomenon of a happy man, and it is a study in blank puzzlement. Frederick is happy, after all, in a way few women are, as if Crusoe's island had found its ultimate example in psychological self-sufficiency. He is complete. A Londoner with a hotel on the Italian Riviera, he will spend by choice a whole day of leisure in Nice, without his wife, serene and alone, doing nothing in particular and with no special purpose in view: 'such a happy man, so elegant, so smiling, as he wends his way down the slippery and sharply descending streets that everyone gives him a greeting: . . . the spirit of the place, if not its patron.' He rejects the advances of any woman, however attractive, since to his mind 'the man offers and the woman gratifies' – to return home to his wife, work a little and smoke a second, last cigar of the day before retiring to bed:

> Strange, how excellent this marriage has proved to be, the man offering, the woman gratifying. . . . Strange, how rooted they appear to be in this frivolous place, divorced from serious need or concern . . . No wonder Frederick never seriously considers going home again.

No wonder indeed. But of course Frederick is altogether a wonder to the feminine consciousness, whether feminist or not. He is happy – happy just as he is; and though few men may be that, even fewer women are. The passage, though elegantly poised, is analytic of a state of confusion and bewilderment. How can it be so? It exemplifies the wondering semi-comprehension through which the sexes contemplate each other: a mutual admiration mixed with sympathy, irritation and moments of sudden alarm; and the pains and pleasures of sex are the least of the matter. That bewildered half-understanding is more accurate, in the end, as a report on experience than any battle between the sexes. There is a congeniality between men and women that is natural and yet never complete. If there has to be a battle between the sexes, as some women have noticed, it is a battle the male is always likely to win, if only because of his self-sufficiency. If he prefers his woman to stay at home, he can persuade her that work is demeaning; if he prefers her to earn, that work is self-fulfilling. There is also, as the age has noticed, a congeniality within a given sex that is all but complete; and it needs no more than a gesture, or the shift of a facial muscle, to be felt. Amis's *Stanley and the Women* ends with a wife who has tried to terrorise her husband into submission phoning to be taken back. Women understand women, it appears, but men also understand men; and the novel ends.

> While she hurried on about having been so desperately frightened and upset, . . . I turned towards Cliff, who did the brief lift of the chin South London people use to mean I told you so or Here we go again or Wouldn't you bleeding know. People elsewhere too, I dare say. Perhaps all over the world.

9

Characters

The literature of Britain has a characteristic strength that lacks almost everything except abundance and gusto. It lacks a name, an identity, an analytical tradition to interpret it, even a literary kind proper to itself.

I shall call it the character, since it deals with individuals rather than species, whether factual, fictional or a mingling of the two. French before English, on the whole, as a literary activity, it is omnipresent in gossip and in learned conversation; and in literature it is so irrepressible that it surfaces in all the literary forms that there are, whether novels, essays, obituaries, letters, diaries, or plays. It can even happen, occasionally, in a poem. It has a certain standing in literary annals, though not the longest or the best defined, being familiar to the seventeenth century in Aubrey's *Brief Lives* or in Clarendon's *History of the Rebellion*. Neither of these, significantly enough, were works published (or meant to be published) in the author's lifetime, since the description of a real character is essentially as indiscreet and dangerous as good gossip. It partly emerges from its secretive life in the eighteenth century, with the periodical essay and the rise of biography as a published form, as in Boswell's *Life of Johnson*; and by the nineteenth century, when Aubrey, Pepys and Evelyn belatedly saw the light of print, it entered into its full strength, in a nation famous for its eccentrics, and assumed a place which, though nameless, is by now more or less taken for granted. In a literature like English, which is poor – relative to its neighbours – in nothing but aphorisms, anecdotes supply a host of aphorisms buried in narrative form, and the character has never flourished so vigorously as in the present century, as in Winston Churchill's *Great Contemporaries* or in the biography-boom and the craze for political memoirs and diaries that followed the Second World War. Given a fiction which, at times, has lost its sense of reality, the character can be an essential link with the real. Everyone knows there is nothing so queer as folks. But the complex reality of social life requires one to be reminded of it, by instances, all the time.

With a famed tradition of eccentricity to justify, the British are plainly and predictably good at characters: at being them, at talking about them, at writing about them. They are masters, for instance, of the obituary. The world's most avid newspaper-readers, they are interested less in news, when they read the daily or weekly press, than in personalities; and when a celebrity dies, radio and television vie with the press to record memories, merry or solemn, about the dead. In 1975 *The Times* began to publish imposing collections of its more notable obituaries, anonymous though they still were, as they had appeared in the daily press: decade by decade, beginning with a volume on the 1960s that included a 13,500-word obituary of Churchill, who had died in January 1965. Like the rest of them, the Churchill obituary was composed in anticipation and largely before the death of its subject, and it represents a palimpsest of revisions over the years by more than one hand. It is a critical panegyric, in essence, combining on a large scale the qualities of narrative, dissection and celebration; and it ends '... he carried to fulfilment a genius that in his father showed only brilliant promise. His renown is assured as long as the story of these lands is told.' But like many anecdotes it is without an author: an unattributable masterpiece.

Character is potent, as a literary idea. When an author is at a loss for subject, he writes one: most usually a memoir, since biography had by the 1960s made itself the most successful of all non-fictional forms. An auto-biography, which is the easiest kind of biography to write, technically speaking, is most commonly a string of remembered characters – parents, friends and ac-quaintances. But the form is radically unfixed. In John Betjeman's poem 'A Subaltern's Love-Song' (1945), which is about a tennis-girl called Miss Joan Hunter Dunn, it hardly matters whether she is an individual or an archetype. John Mortimer's play *A Voyage round my Father* (1971) is loosely built around the dramatist's own father, a blind solicitor who worked on without ever admitting his crushing disability; and Laurie Lee's *Cider with Rosie* (1959) is an unplanned, freewheeling recollec-tion of a village childhood in Gloucestershire, only slowly taking shape, if it ever does, as it moves towards the final, riotous scene of a boy's seduction by a village girl in the woods while drunk with cider. But much of the foreground of the book is occupied by an eccentric mother, poor but with a profound instinct for finery and old porcelain – 'a servant girl born to silk' – with reverent memories of the life of the gentry she had once served. When her absent, errant, faithless husband dies, she follows him fast into lunacy and then death:

She had raised his two families, faithfully and alone: had waited thirty-five years for his praise. And through all that time she had clung to one fantasy – that aged and broken, at last in need, he might one day return to her. His death killed that promise, and also ended her reason ... She became frail, simple-minded, and returned to her youth, to that girlhood which had never known him. She never mentioned him again, but spoke to shadows, saw visions, and then she died (p. 162).

★   ★   ★

Character is classically a mixed mode. Though it tells stories it is essentially non-narrative, being concerned with achieving a portrait to be taken and savoured at a glance. It begins in history, usually recent history, as in Aubrey's *Lives* or in the series of telling portraits that interrupt the unsteady flow of Clarendon's history of the English Civil War; and by the twentieth century, if not sooner, it straddles the boundaries of fact and fiction. In her *Balkan Trilogy* (1960–5), for example, Olivia Manning based the eccentric Yakimov, a brandy-sodden raconteur in Bucharest, half Irish and half White Russian, on a Scotsman of her early acquaintance, striving hard as a novelist to cover her tracks by altering his nationality and a good deal else; but to the end of her days she remained alarmed that he, or his friends, might notice the resemblance. Other debts are avowed or self-evident. No reader needs to be told that Muriel Spark based the heroine of *The Prime of Miss Jean Brodie* (1961) on an Edinburgh schoolmistress she had known as a girl; and in his preface to *The Honourable Schoolboy* (1977) John le Carré candidly admits that the character of Crew is based on 'the great Dick Hughes, whose outward character and mannerisms I have shamelessly exaggerated'. Such shame is sometimes easily admitted and as easily forgotten. Sometimes a place can usurp the role of an individual being, as in Elizabeth Bowen's *A Time in Rome* (1960), where an ancient city, endless of interest, becomes the object of an extended and loving contemplation, as if of a friend: 'My darling, my darling, my darling,' the book ends, as if a great city had achieved personality; and with personality, the passion of love.

A novel, too can be an extended character, and the character can even be the novelist himself. Evelyn Waugh's *The Ordeal of Gilbert Pinfold* (1957), which appeared when he was fifty-four, tells of a famous novelist of fifty, the author of a dozen books still read and valued who, like Waugh himself, had retired to live in the country:

> affectionate, high-spirited and busy in childhood; dissipated and often despairing in youth; sturdy and prosperous in early manhood; he had in middle age degenerated less than many of his contemporaries,

attributing that modest superiority to his 'long, lonely, tranquil days' in a village a hundred miles from London, till there came upon him unawares the alarming hallucinations attendant on a nervous breakdown – a breakdown which, as Waugh must have guessed, was already known to his friends and would some day be reported in faithful detail by his biographers. So characters can be fact or fiction, or they can be fact and fiction at the same time; and the reader can be meant to guess, or forbidden to guess – or, as in an obituary, simply told that he is reading a just account of a real original. It may be convenient, then, for a moment, to treat the character, central as it is to so much conversation and literature of the age, whether historical or fictional, as if it were a single and unitary form.

★   ★   ★

Like buildings, characters have insides and outsides; and to know one in life or in a book is to guess, or try to guess, how the inner being relates to the outer shell of appearance, to voice and gesture, and how mannerisms reveal (or fail to reveal) a hidden life of being. Such acquaintances need not be intimate. They can be casual or occasional – an intuitive act that can operate even through brick walls. 'We were in Sherborne this afternoon,' Sylvia Townsend Warner once wrote in a private letter:

> It was raining, and in one of the half-holiday classrooms a boy was practising the trumpet ... – the pleasure and rapture of playing it. Every note said so. Such flourishes! Such offended blackbird's squawks![1]

It must be supposed the novelist never met the boy; but the incident could be the start of a story, of an essay or of a play, perhaps on the genius of youth and its outcome, happy or sad. Left as a letter, it is character at its most insignificant and casual; at its most developed, it can be the summary of an acquaintance, above all a long-enjoyed friendship, where tell-tale mannerisms – a lift of the voice, perhaps, or a repeated gesture – provide a rich clue to an inner being. 'There was a gesture of his I shall never forget,' a colleague once wrote of a dead professor in a college obituary:

> It was the sudden assumption of a new posture and mien; his slender back, always upright, was held even straighter, his shoulders were thrown back, his hands too, so that his chin came forward, and one saw that he might well be formidable ... It was the very gesture of a man squaring up to something that mattered, despite his lack of an inch or two. And for the moment, his stature was formidable.[2]

That is to share a puzzle about personality: how is it that little people, even if they are not actors, can suddenly make themselves look big? Presumably there is something in them larger than their outsides imply. The character of a friend, above all, is an intimate paradox, since it contains multiple incompatibilities and contradictions. To know more is to understand less, sometimes, but because of its intimacy such knowledge is a puzzle profoundly rewarding to the imagination and teasing to thought. 'His arm is outstretched towards me,' C. H. Rolph ended his memoir of his old friend Kingsley Martin, whose portrait (warts and all) he had elaborately drawn in *Kingsley* (1973), recalling the behaviour of his old editor at the office door as he would stand there, in days gone by, eager for copy:

> his fingers are snapping, his heavy-lidded eyes have gone unusually circular with agitation and astonishment. I seem to hand him the manuscript, which he almost snatches. But as soon as it is in his hand, his face softens. Even without looking at it, he nods at me several times with a wide and tight-lipped grin, looking again rather like Mr Punch; and he goes away. I wish he had not gone away.

The ambiguity of that last, short, monosyllabic period makes of the book an elegy for a dead friend, recalled as if in a dream and ingeniously presented as a biography.

This is an omnipresent form. The spread of character across the literary kinds of British literature is matched by its spread across a range of emotions, which is apparently limitless. It can be written out of hatred, detachment or love. It can be realistic or fantasising, as Sylvia Townsend Warner once fantasised about the musical schoolboy she heard but never saw, or as Kingsley Martin's friend fantasised over a dead editor as if over someone once glimpsed in a vision '... I seem to hand him the manuscript': the narrator himself uncertain whether the recollection of a friend who left so much to forgive was itself, by then, imaginative or real.

★   ★   ★

Character is secretive, especially in the life of an introspective people tending towards an inward self-sufficiency; and to write of character, at its most profound, is to attempt to solve a puzzle or unravel a secret. The life of Kingsley Martin of the *New Statesman* was such a puzzle, in the sense that all self-contradictory natures are puzzling; and at its richest literary extension, the exercise can be a prolonged entertainment of contradictions where riddles are contemplated and left intriguingly unresolved. How can people be like that, talk like that, behave like that? Such questions are the stuff of ignorant conversation and of great literature alike, of Boswell's *Life of Johnson* and the mass of journalism that lies in the middle ground between good talk and literature. The life of the nation is unimaginable without it.

An author tending to a Crusoe-like self-sufficiency in his own life may have more than one reason for attempting a character. The commonest reason, perhaps, and the most practical, is that an acquaintance may present him with materials present and ready-made. There may, in addition, be an unspoken reason, and a more private one: that to write about others exempts from the task of writing, even thinking, about oneself. Self-knowledge, in any case, is hard to have, harder still to impart; autobiography may be easy to write, but it is not easy to get right, and damaging if you do; and the character, considered a literary exercise, can be a form of reticence. The most public and rational motive here concerns the strategies one contrives in order to live and prosper in a world made by others. To learn about the inhabited world is to learn about others – their mysteries, their secrets and their follies. Parents, to begin with, are always fair game, at least once they are dead: they are at once familiar and mystifying. When Nigel Nicolson, on the death of his mother Vita Sackville-West in 1962, discovered a locked Gladstone bag in the corner of her sitting-room, cut it open and found her autobiography there, to be published as *Portrait of a Marriage* (1973), he did something more than contribute a new instalment to the long-running saga of bisexual Bloomsbury revelations. He explained, both to himself and to the world, at least in some degree, how his parents could have been at once happily married and yet unfaithful – early and often in their married life – and with lovers of the same sex: 'Marriage and sex could be quite different things.' The mystery of desire is not resolved by such a book, but it is rendered more manageable. And beyond parents, there are the friends of one's youth, remembered over the years. John Wain's characters of authors he has known, though composed decades apart, are thoughtful, brooding studies of a trade that is well known to be psychologically dangerous: the first a study in failure, the other in the arrogance of success.

E. H. W. Meyerstein was a friend of Wain's undergraduate years at Oxford, Marshall McLuhan of his early independent manhood. Both essays, in their separate ways, are studies in affectionate bafflement. There was a great deal in Meyerstein's behaviour, which oscillated between simplicity and paranoia, that his young friend found 'utterly baffling': immensely learned, and the author of over twenty books, rich and well connected, the man, even beyond his presumed homosexuality, was possessed of a secret sorrow:

> It is only when I look back that I see it at all clearly – the tragic disappointment, the sense of heaving away for years at a weight too heavy to lift, the deep frost that had settled on his hopes.

Bombed out of his London rooms during the Blitz, snubbed (as he believed) by the dons of his old Oxford college – 'Oxford has worlds to offer, but not to those who ask' – and above all humiliated by the sheer indignity of his physical oddity:

> He was clumsy and awkward; his voice was hoarse in its deep register, and rose to a grating shriek when he became excited; he never mastered the art of shaving, so that there were always tufts of stiff, greyish hair sticking out from odd portions of his face . . . And yet . . . there was a lightness and grace about some of his movements – particularly, as I have said, with the hands; intelligence and imagination flashed from his eyes . . . He was not one of those people who give the impression that they would be happier without bodies.[3]

That is to share a question rather than to answer it. Or there was Marshall McLuhan, the Canadian theorist, always talking, always theorising, 'pouring out the continuous stream of notions that issued from his ceaselessly active mind like an unstoppable flow of ticker-tape . . .'[4] Many points are well scored here. And yet, in the end, as with Samuel Johnson's *Life of Savage*, the reader is left occasionally to feel that he understands such characters better than friendship has allowed the author himself to understand them. Character, at its best, is open-ended. It was not Establishment anti-semitism that caused Meyerstein to fail as an author, one tentatively concludes, but his own literary mediocrity. And in the study of McLuhan a portrait of intellectual arrogance, of spoiling by success, is drawn in a manner too detailed and too fine to end in a verdict, though to the reader a verdict is still blindingly clear.

Perhaps the ultimate fascination of character – of real character – lies beyond simple judgement. It is a form full, by its very nature, of the unfabricated, the raw, the unarranged. Other people, it says, are not just different from oneself. They are different, sometimes, beyond all imagining. They achieve an impressive and enviable absurdity, and one can only note them wonderingly and admire. Bruce Chatwin opens his travel-book *Songlines* (1987) with the portrait of a man he met in central Australia, a son of Russian immigrants who busies himself with tracing the invisible paths or songlines which, as the aborigines believe, were walked by legendary beings who sang the names of things as they walked and created the world as they sang. The young man who dedicates himself to that esoteric pursuit of knowledge owns hardly anything in his remote desert home but a harpsichord and a shelf of books, and when he returns from his hundred-mile walks he draws the curtain and plays Buxtehude and Bach to himself. No novelist, surely, would attempt such a figure. It is beyond mere eccentricity. It demands no comment, allows none, and gets none. Other people are irreducibly and imposingly wonderful.

And that, no doubt, is why character is in the last resort indispensable. Mere stories, and especially fictional stories, have proved too tidy to tell the whole of life: too confined and constrained, too eager to see a point and make a point, too self-evidently contrived. No novelists would dare invent the life of Churchill, as his obituarists must have known; or the spy-stories, more or less true, that fill the daily and weekly newspapers; or the original beings you meet on a journey or overhear on a bus. Achieving the absurd needs to be true, after all, to count. Invention is easy, but truth, like a condiment, enlivens whatever it touches. And the fiercest fascination offered by character, in the end, is the knowledge that such beings are living beings, their secrets ultimately unfathomable, their triumphs and failures real.

Notes and References

1: CRUSOE'S ISLAND

1. David Jones, *Anathemata* (London, 1952), preface.
2. Kathleen Tynan, *The Life of Kenneth Tynan* (London, 1987), p. 117.
3. Philip Larkin, 'The Blending of Betjeman' (1960), in his *Required Writing* (London, 1983), p. 129.
4. A. Alvarez, 'Beyond the Gentility Principle', *Observer* (19 February 1961); revised in his Penguin anthology *The New Poetry* (Harmondsworth, 1962) and in his *Beyond All This Fribble* (London, 1968), p. 38.
5. Colin Wilson, 'My First Book', *The Author* (Autumn 1986).
6. BBC Radio 4, 9 November 1986.

2: ORWELL/WAUGH

1. George Orwell, *Collected Essays, Journalism and Letters* (London, 1968), IV.513.
2. Evelyn Waugh, *Tablet* (6 April 1946); reprinted in his *Essays, Articles and Reviews* (London, 1983), p. 305.
3. Anthony Powell, 'George Orwell: A Memoir', *Atlantic Monthly* (October 1967), p. 65.
4. Orwell, *Collected Essays, Journalism and Letters* (1968) IV. 438, from a letter to Julian Symons.
5. Malcolm Muggeridge, 'A Knight of the Woeful Countenance', in *The World of George Orwell*, edited by Miriam Gross (London, 1971), p. 173.
6. Evelyn Waugh, 'An Act of Homage and Reparation to P. G. Wodehouse', *Sunday Times* (16 July 1961); reprinted in his *Essays, Articles and Reviews* (1983), p. 563.
7. Evelyn Waugh, 'Two Unquiet Lives', *Tablet* (5 May 1951); reprinted in his *Essays, Articles and Reviews* (1983), p. 395.
8. George Orwell, 'Tobias Smollett', *Tribune* (22 September 1944); reprinted in his *Collected Essays, Journalism and Letters* (London, 1968), III.248.
9. *Radio Times*, 18–24 April 1987.

3: CHRISTIAN REVIVAL: TOLKIEN AND LEWIS

1. C. S. Lewis, *Letters*, edited by W. H. Lewis (London, 1966), pp. 287, 288, from a letter of 15 May 1959.
2. Ibid., p. 268, from a letter of 13 March 1956.
3. Humphrey Carpenter, *The Inklings* (London, 1978), pp. 65–6.
4. J. R. R. Tolkien, *Letters*, edited by Humphrey Carpenter (London, 1981), p. 218, from a letter of June 1955.
5. John Wain, *Sprightly Running* (London, 1962), p. 180.
6. C. S. Lewis, *Letters* (1966), p. 226, from a letter of January 1951.
7. C. S. Lewis, 'A Reply to Professor Haldane', in his *Of This and Other Worlds* (London, 1982), p. 103.

4: THE CORONATION OF REALISM

1. 'In the Movement', *Spectator* (1 October 1954), an anonymous article by J. D. Scott, the literary editor, who later publicly revealed his authorship in *Spectator* (16 April 1977). See also Bernard Bergonzi, 'From the Fifties to the Seventies', *Critical Quarterly* (Spring 1973), who sees the Movement as marked by a shift from fee-paying schooling to free grammar schools; and Blake Morrison, *The Movement* (London, 1980).
2. *Sunday Times* (25 December 1955).
3. *Why Do I Write?: An Exchange of Views between Elizabeth Bowen, Graham Greene and V. S. Pritchett* (London, 1948), p. 30.
4. Ibid., p. 49.
5. F. P. W. McDowell, 'An Interview with Angus Wilson', *Iowa Review* 3 (1972); reprinted in Angus Wilson, *Diversity and Depth in Fiction* (London, 1983), p. 265.
6. Malcolm Bradbury, 'Return of the Angry Old Turk', *The Times* (17 May 1984).
7. Kingsley Amis, 'My Kind of Comedy', *Twentieth Century* (July 1961), p. 50.
8. William Golding, *Nobel Lecture 7 December 1983* (London, 1984), unpaged.
9. T. S. Eliot, *Knowledge and Experience in the Philosophy of F. H. Bradley* (London, 1964), p. 159.
10. *Independent* (26 January 1989).

11. Kingsley Amis, 'A Man on Rockall', *Spectator* (6 November 1956).

12. Iris Murdoch, 'Against Dryness', *Encounter* (January 1961); reprinted in *The Novel Today*, edited by Malcolm Bradbury (London, 1977), p. 27.

13. Frank Kermode, 'The House of Fiction: Interviews with Seven English Novelists', *Partisan Review* 30 (1963), the seven being Iris Murdoch, Graham Greene, Angus Wilson, Ivy Compton-Burnett, C. P. Snow, John Wain, and Muriel Spark.

14. Ibid.

15. Iris Murdoch, 'Mass, Might and Myth,' *Spectator* (7 September 1962).

16. *Men of Ideas*, edited by Bryan Magee (London: BBC, 1978), pp. 226–7.

17. Kingsley Amis, 'My Kind of Comedy', *Twentieth Century* (July 1961), p. 48.

18. Frank Kermode, 'Remembering the Movement and Researching It', *London Review of Books* (5–18 June 1980), who characterises the 1950s Movement as Buskellite, or situated on the Conservative–Labour overlap, 'with a preference for the But end of the term,' which may be a little over-mild.

19. *Conviction*, edited by Norman Mackenzie (London, 1958), p. 218.

20. Iris Murdoch, 'Against Dryness', *Encounter* (January 1961); reprinted in *The Novel Today*, edited by Malcolm Bradbury (London 1977), p. 30. See also her 'The Sublime and the Beautiful Revisited', *Yale Review* 49 (1960).

21. Iris Murdoch, *Conviction*, edited by Norman MacKenzie (London, 1958), p. 228.

22. Philip Larkin, *Required Writing* (London, 1983), p. 64, from a *Paris Review* interview of 1982.

23. Iris Murdoch, 'The Sublime and the Beautiful Revisited', *Yale Review* 49 (1960), p. 262.

24. Iris Murdoch, ibid.

5: A CRITICAL MOMENT

1. John Wain, 'The Vanishing Critic', in his *A House for the Truth* (London, 1972), pp. 28–9.

2. Editorial in *Mandrake* (Oxford) (Summer–Autumn 1953),

when the journal, founded by John Wain in 1945, was edited by the poet Arthur Boyars.

3. 'William Empson in Conversation with Christopher Ricks', *The Review* (June 1963), p. 26.

4. William Empson, 'Curds and Whey', *Granta* (11 May 1928); reprinted in his *Argufying*, edited by John Haffenden (London, 1987), p. 69.

5. Empson, *Argufying* (1987), p. 517.

6. Empson, 'The Queen and I', *London Review of Books* (26 November 1987). See also his highly autobiographical Sheffield inaugural of 1953, 'Teaching English in the Far East', ibid. (17 August 1989).

7. Empson, *Argufying* (1987) pp. 28–9, from a letter to Frank Kermode of 27 March 1961.

8. F. R. Leavis, 'A New "Establishment" in Criticism?', *Listener* (1 November 1956); reprinted in his *Letters in Criticism*, edited by John Tasker (London, 1974), p. 54.

9. Denys Thompson, letter to the *Guardian* (24 July 1973).

10. Raymond Williams, 'Culture is Ordinary', in *Conviction*, edited by Norman Mackenzie (London, 1958), p. 81.

11. Donald Davie, in *My Cambridge*, edited by Ronald Hayman (London, 1977), p. 87.

12. *Peter Hall's Diaries*, edited by John Goodwin (London, 1983), p. 347, 18 April 1978, on hearing of the death of Leavis.

13. C. S. Lewis, 'Unreal Estates', in his *Of This and Other Worlds* (London, 1982), p. 191.

14. Lewis, 'Shelley and Mr. Eliot' in his *Rehabilitations* (Oxford, 1939); 'Metre' (1960) in his *Selected Literary Essays* (Cambridge, 1969).

15. *English Literature in the Sixteenth Century* (Oxford, 1954), p. 32.

16. Ibid., p. 221.

17. Frank Kermode, 'William Golding' (1964); reprinted in his *Modern Essays* (London, 1971), p. 239.

6: POETS

1. Donald Davie, *These the Companions* (Cambridge, 1982), p. 141.

2. Davie, *The Poet in the Imaginary Museum* (Manchester, 1977), p. 67.

3. Geoffrey Hill, in *Viewpoints: Poets in Conversation*, edited by John Haffenden (London, 1981), pp. 88, 99.
4. Dylan Thomas, *Quite Early One Morning: broadcasts* (London, 1954), pp. 125–6.
5. Thomas Gunn, 'Writing a Poem' in his *Occasions of Poetry* (London, 1982), p. 152.
6. Philip Larkin, 'Aubade', *TLS* (23 December 1977); reprinted in his *Collected Poems*, edited by Anthony Thwaite (London, 1988), pp. 208–9.
7. Larkin, 'Wanted: Good Hardy Critic' (1966); reprinted in his *Required Writing: miscellaneous pieces 1955–82* (London, 1983), p. 174.
8. Larkin, *Required Writing* (1983), p. 67, from a 1982 interview; 'What's Become of Wystan?' (1960), ibid., pp. 123–8.
9. Larkin, 'Breadfruit', *Critical Quarterly* (Winter 1961); reprinted in his *Collected Poems* (London, 1988), p. 141.
10. Thomas Gunn, *The Occasions of Poetry* (1982), pp. 106–7.
11. Ibid., p. 156.

7: OSBORNE, PINTER, STOPPARD

1. Shaun Sutton, *The Largest Theatre in the World: thirty years of television drama* (London: BBC, 1982).
2. George Lyttleton to Rupert Hart-Davis (25 June 1959), in *The Lyttleton–Hart-Davis Letters* (London, 1982), IV.86.
3. Kenneth Tynan, *Curtains* (London, 1961), p. 130.
4. Martin Esslin, 'Letter to Peter Wood [by] Harold Pinter', *Kenyon Review* new ser. 3 (1981).
5. Lawrence M. Bensky, 'Harold Pinter: An Interview', *Paris Review* 39 (1966).
6. Renford Bambrough, 'G. E. Moore in Conversation', *Listener* (20 May 1971), based on a 1957 broadcast interview with Moore on Bertrand Russell's ideas about memory.
7. *Sunday Times* (25 February 1968).

9: CHARACTERS

1. Sylvia Townsend Warner, *Letters*, edited by William Maxwell (London, 1982), p. viii, from a letter of 30 June 1953.
2. Hugh Sykes Davies, 'Norman Brooke Jopson', *The Eagle* (Cambridge) 63 (1969), p. 68.

3. John Wain, *Sprightly Running* (London, 1962), p. 111.
4. Wain, *Dear Shadows: Portraits from Memory* (London, 1986), p. 77.

Index

Books on regular loan may be checked out for four weeks. Books must be presented at the Circulation Desk in order to be renewed.

A fine is charged after date due.

Special books are subject to special regulations at the discretion of the library staff.